JAPANE
ENGLISH-JAPANESE
Romanized

HIPPOCRENE CONCISE DICTIONARY

JAPANESE-ENGLISH
ENGLISH-JAPANESE
Romanized

Ikuko Anjo

HIPPOCRENE BOOKS
New York

Third printing, 2001

For information, contact:
HIPPOCRENE BOOKS, INC.
171 Madison Avenue
New York, NY 10016

Library of Congress Cataloging-in-Publication Data
Anjo, Ikuko.
     Hippocrene concise dictionary, Japanese-English/
    English-Japanese (romanized) / Ikuko Anjo.
          p.   cm.
    ISBN 0-7818-0162-1
    1. Japanese language--Dictionaries--English. 2. En-
    glish language-Dictionaries--Japanese. I. Title.
    PL679.A476   1993
    495.6'321--dc293-24118

                                  CIP

Printed in the United States of America.

Introduction

According to a report published by the Educational Testing Service[1], in order to reach average speaking proficiency in Japanese, it requires 2400-2760 hours as compared with French and Spanish (720 hours) or Greek and Hebrew (1320 hours). Isn't it challenging to study Japanese? Life is no fun without a challenging spirit! Only if you have interest, patience and diligence, will you be able to master Japanese.

Speaking of my six-year experience in teaching Japanese at the U.S. Office of Naval Research in Tokyo, American scientists, who worked in the field of mathematics, physics and computer systems, agreed that the Japanese language was very mathematical and not difficult to gain oral proficiency. That's right! It is not difficult. Please forget the myth that Japanese is difficult. It is only different.

This English-Japanese/Japanese-English dictionary is comprised of approximately 8000 words and a source of everyday expressions. It is written in English and romanized Japanese for your convenience; however, you might encourage yourself to learn the Japanese writing system (Kanji, Hiraganan and Katakana) which will gradually take you into the enchanting world of the Japanese language.

For those who are students, tourists, businessmen and others who wish to carry a compact handy dictionary, this one is for you. Good luck!

Ikuko Anjo
Stamford, CT.
April, 1993

1. Judith E. Liskin-Gasparro. ETS Oral Proficiency Testing Manual. Princeton, N.J.: Educational Testing Service, 1982.

Before You Use This Dictionary: Fundamentals to Remember

1. Abbreviations

(n.)	noun
(pron.)	pronoun
(prep.)	preposition
(v.)	verb
(adj.)	adjective
(adv.)	adverb
(conj.)	conjunction
(aux.v.)	auxiliary verb
(attrib.)	attributive
(int.)	interjection

* These abbreviations are marked only when the word can be mistaken with another meaning.

2. Signs

—   double duration

e.g.   ō is to be pronounced for twice as long as o.

In n´a, for example, n and a are to be pronounced separately. Therefore, n´a is distinguished from the the single syllable na.

3. Accent

The Japanese accent known as "pitch accent" is different from "stress accent" in English. In Japanese, instead of pronouncing a syllable louder, one or more beats of a word are pronounced at a higher pitch than the rest. In this dictionary, accent is marked with — or ⌐ over a syllable or syllables and only in case there are two or more homonyms appeared next to each other.

e.g.   denki   electricity
         denki   biography

4. Pronunciation

(1) a   like a in common or partner

e	like e in met or kettle
i	like i in mill or win
o	like o in cost or boss
u	like u in put or book

(2)

b	like b in beer or butter
d	like d in deer or day
g	like g in good or singer
h	like h in hum or home
j	like j in jam or jog
k	like k in keep or kind
m	like m in mind or meet
n	like n in nap or nest
p	like p in palm or plant
r	like l in lily or lay
s	like s in summer or stamp
t	like t in tear or table
w	like w in Washington or want
z	like z in zone or zoo
y	like y in young or york

* The sound g is pronounced as a velar nasal like nga, unless it is the initial letter of the word.
* Before p, b and m, n is pronounced as m.
* The sound r is rather closer to English l than r.
* The diphthongs ei and ii are usually pronounced just like ē and Ī.
* The following clusters are pronounced as one syllable: by, ch, gy, hy, ky, my, ny, py, ry, sh and ts.

(3) Words with double consonant such as cch, kk, ss, tt, ttsu need special attention to make its meaning clear. In kitte, for example, the first t is actually devocalized, instead, a pause, which is almost as long as any other voiced syllable, is made.

e.g.   icchi(i·c·chi)   agreement
       ichi(i·chi)   location or position

gakku (ga·k·ku)	school district
gaku (ga·ku)	frame
kesshō (ke·s·sho)	crystal
keshō (ke·sho)	make-up
kitte (ki·t·te)	postage stamp
kite (ki·te)	te-form of kuru which means come
mittsu (mi·t·tsu)	three
mitsu (mi·tsu)	honey

5. Others

    (1) You need (na) or (no) after the adjective when a noun follows.

        <u>e.g.</u> shizuka (na)   shizuka<u>na</u> umi (quiet sea)

             naimitsu (no)   naimitsu <u>no</u> hanashi

                               (confidential conversation)

    (2) In a Japanese word, a hyphen is used only when it is needed to make the meaning clear and easy to read.

        <u>e.g.</u> dai-kyōkoku (canyon)

             unten-menkyoshō (driver's license)

A.	abacus	soroban
	abalone	awabi
	abandon	(v.) suteru; dan'nen suru
	abbreviation	ryakugo
	ability	nōryoku
	able	kanō(na); nōryoku no aru
	abortion	ninshin-chūzetsu
	about	(prep.) ...ni tsuite
		(adv.) oyoso; yaku
	above	(prep.) yori takaku
		(adj.) zenjutsu(no)
		(adv.) ue ni
	abridge	tanshuku suru; yōyaku suru
	abroad	kaigai ni; gaikoku de
	abrupt	totsuzen(no); bukkirabō(na)
	abruptly	kyū ni
	absence	kesseki; huzai
	absent	kesseki(no); huzai(no)
	absent-minded	bonyarishita
	absolute	zettai(no); kanpeki(na)
	absolutely	mattaku; tashika ni
	abstract	(adj.) chūshōteki(na)
		(n.) yōyaku
	abundant	hōhu(na)
	abuse	(v.) ranyō suru; gyakutai suru
		(n.) ranyō; gyakutai
	academic	(adj.) gakumonteki(na); gakuen(no)
	accent	(n.) akusento; kuchō
	accept	ukeireru; uketoru
	acceptable	ukeirerareru; konomashii
	accident	jiko
	accidental	(adj.) huryo(no); gūzen(no)
	accommodate	shukuhaku saseru; shūyō dekiru
	accommodation	shukuhaku-setsubi; tekiō

accompany	tomonau
accomplish	nashitogeru
according to	...ni yoru to
accountant	kaikeishi; kaikei-gakari
accumulate	tsumiageru; tsumoru
accurate	seikaku(na)
accuse	hinan suru; kokuhatsu suru
accustom	shūkanzukeru
ache	(v.) itamu
	(n.) itami
achieve	nashitogeru
acid	(n.) san
	(adj.) sanmi no aru
acknowledge	mitomeru; uketotta-koto o shiraseru; kansha suru
acquaintance	shiriai
acquire	shūtoku suru; kakutoku suru
across	(adv.) yokogitte
act	(v.) kōdo suru; jikkō suru; enjiru
active	katsudōteki(na)
actor	haiyū
actual	jissai(no)
actually	jissai ni
acupuncture	(n.) hari-ryōji
adapt	tekiō saseru; jun'nō suru
add	kuwaeru
addict	(n.) chūdokusha; jōyōsha
address	(n.) jūsho; enzetsu
adequate	tekitō(na); jūbun(na)
adjective	(n.) keiyōshi
adjoin	rinsetsu suru
adjust	tekiō suru; awaseru
administration	kanri; keiei; gyōsei
admire	shōsan suru; kantan suru
admission	nyūjō; nyūgaku
admit	mitomeru; kyoka suru
adolescence	seishunki

adopt	yōshi ni suru; (iken, hōshin nado o) saiyō suru
adorable	kawairashii
adore	sūhai suru; netsuai suru
adult	(n.) otona
advanced	jōkyū(no); susunda
advantage	(n.) rieki; riten
advantageous	yūri(na)
adventure	(n.) bōken
adverb	hukushi
advertisement	kōkoku
advice	jogen; chūkoku
advise	jogen suru; chūkoku suru
adviser	sōdanyaku; komon
aerogram	kōkū-shokan
affair	gyōmu; jiken
affect	eikyō o oyobosu
affection	aijō
affectionate	aijō no komotta
affirmative	(adj.) kōteiteki(na)
	(n.) kōtei
affluent	hōhu(na); huyū(na)
afford	yoyū ga aru
afraid	osorete; shinpaishite
Africa	Ahurika
after	(prep.) ...no ato ni; ...no ato de
	(adv.) ato ni
	(conj.) ...shita ato de
after all	kekkyoku
afternoon	gogo
afterward	ato de; sono go
After you	Dōzo osaki ni.
again	hutatabi
again and again	nandomo
against	(prep.) ...ni hantaishite; ...ni taishite
age	(n.) nenrei; jidai
agenda	gidai

aggressive	kōgekiteki(na); sekkyokuteki(na)
ago	...mae ni
agree	sansei suru
agreeable	kokoroyoi; tekitō(na)
agreement	dōi; kyōtei
agriculture	nōgyō
ahead	saki ni; saki e; ikute ni
aid	(v.) enjo suru
	(n.) enjo; kyūen
aim	(v.) nerau; mezasu
	(n.) mokuteki; mato
air	(n.) kūki; yōsu
air mail	kōkūbin
airplane	hikōki
airport	kūkō
aisle	tsūro
alarm clock	mezamashi-dokei
album	arubamu
alcohol	sake; arukōru
algebra	daisū
alike	niteiru
alive	ikiteiru
all	(adj.) subete(no)
	(adv.) sukkari
allergy	arerugī
alligator	wani
allow	yurusu; kyoka suru
allowance	teate; kozukai
all right	kekkō; yoroshii
alma mater	bokō
almanac	nenkan; koyomi
almost	hotondo; mō sukoshi de
alone	(adj.) hitori de; tada...dake de
	(adv.) hitori de; dokuryoku de
along	(prep.) ...ni sotte
	(adv.) ...to issho ni; ...ni sotte

aloud	koe o dashite
already	sude ni
also	(adv.) ...mo mata; sarani
	(conj.) sono ue
alter	kaeru
alternative	(adj.) kawari(no); nisha-takuitsu(no)
although	daga; towaie
altitude	hyōkō
altogether	(adv.) zenbu de
alumni	dōsōsei; sotsugyōsei
always	itsumo
a.m.	gozen
amaze	odorokasu
amazing	odorokubeki
ambassador	taishi
ambiguous	aimai(na)
ambition	yashin; taishi
ambulance	kyūkyūsha
America	Amerika
American	(n.) Amerikajin
	(adj.) Amerika(no)
amicable	yūkōteki(na); heiwa(na)
among	(prep.) ...no aida ni; ...no aida de; ...ni majitte
amount	(n.) ryō; kingaku
ample	hiroi; jūbun(na)
amuse	tanoshimaseru
amusement park	yūenchi
analyze	bunseki suru
ancestor	sosen
ancient	mukashi(no)
and	(conj.) soshite; to; sorede; shikashi
and yet	sorenano ni
anecdote	itsuwa; kidan
angel	tenshi
anger	ikari
angle	kakudo

angry	hara o tateta
animal	dōbutsu
animate	(adj.) ikiteiru; kakki no aru
ankle	ashikubi
annex	(n.) bekkan
anniversary	(n.) kinenbi
announce	shiraseru; happyō suru
annoy	komaraseru; iraira-saseru
annual	(adj.) kōrei(no); ichinenkan(no)
anonymous	tokumei(no); sakusha-humei(no)
another	(adj.) mō hitotsu(no); mō hitori(no); betsu(no)
answer	(n.) kotae
	(v.) kotaeru
ant	ari
anthropology	jinruigaku
antibiotic	(n.) kōsei-busshitsu
anticipate	yosō suru; ate ni suru
anticipation	yosō; kitai; yokan
antique	(n.) kottōhin
antonym	han´igo
anxiety	huan; setsubō
anxious	shinpai(na); setsubōshite
any	(adj.) don´na...demo; sukoshimo...nai; ikuraka no
	(adv.) ikuraka; zenzen
anybody	(pron.) daremo; dareka; daredemo
anyhow	dōshitemo; tonikaku
anymore	ima wa mō...de nai
anything	(pron.) nanika; nanimo
anyway	tonikaku
anywhere	dokoka ni; dokonimo
apartment	apāto
apologize	ayamaru
apparel	ihuku
apparent	akiraka(na)
appeal	(v.) uttaeru
appear	arawareru; ...no yōda

appearance	gaikan; shutsugen
appetite	shokuyoku
applaud	hakushu o suru
applause	hakushu
apple	ringo
appliance	kigu; sōchi
application	gansho; shinseisho
apply	mōshikomu; tekiyō suru
appointment	yakusoku; ninmei
appreciate	hyōka suru; kanshō suru; kansha suru
appreciation	kansha; kanshō
apprehensive	huan (na)
approach	(v.) chikazuku
	(n.) sekkin
appropriate	(adj.) tekisetsu (na)
approval	sansei
approve	sansei suru
approximately	oyoso; yaku
April	shigatsu
apt	...shigachi de aru; husawashii
aquarium	suizokukan; suisō
Arab	Arabu
Arabic	(n.) Arabiago
	(adj.) Arabu (no)
archeology	kōkogaku
architect	kenchikuka
architecture	kenchiku
area	chiiki; kuiki
argue	giron suru
argument	giron
arise	okoru; arawareru
arithmetic	(n.) sansū
arm	(n.) ude; buki
armchair	hijikake-isu
army	guntai; rikugun
aroma	hōkō; kaori

around	(adv.) shūhen ni; kaitenshite
	(prep.) ...no mawari ni; ...no achikochi o; oyoso
arrange	totonoeru; junbi suru
arrangement	seiri; junbi
arrest	(v.) taiho suru
arrival	tōchaku
arrive	tōchaku suru
arrogant	gōman(na)
arrow	ya; yajirushi
art	geijutsu; bijutsu
article	kiji; shinamono; ronbun
articulate	(adj.) meikaku(na)
artificial	jinkō(no); mozō(no)
artist	geijutsuka
artistic	geijutsuteki(na)
as	(adv.) ...to onajikurai; ...no yōni
	(conj.) ...hodo; ...to dōyō; ...shita toki; ...nanode
ascend	noboru; agaru
ash	hai
ashamed	hajite; hazukashikute...suru ki ni narenai
Asia	Ajia
Asian	(n.) Ajiajin
	(adj.) Ajia(no)
aside	(adv.) waki ni; betsu ni shite
ask	tazuneru; tanomu
asleep	(adj.) nemutte
assembly	shūkai; kaigi
assert	dangen suru; shuchō suru
assertive	dangenteki(na); gōin(na)
assess	hyōka suru
assign	wariateru
assignment	shukudai
assist	enjo suru; tetsudau
assistant	kyōryokusha; joshu
assume	katei suru
assure	hoshō suru; dangen suru

asthma	zensoku
astonish	odorokasu
astronaut	uchū-hikōshi
astronomy	tenmongaku
athletic	undō-senshurashii; undō-kyōgi(no)
Atlantic Ocean	Taiseiyō
atlas	chizuchō
atomic	genshi(no)
atomosphere	hun'iki; taiki
attach	tsukeru; soeru
attack	(n.) kōgeki
	(v.) kōgeki suru
attempt	(n.) kokoromi
	(v.) kokoromiru
attend	shusseki suru; sewa o suru
attendance	shusseki; tsukisoi
attention	chūi; sewa
attitude	taido
attorney	bengoshi
attract	hikitsukeru
attractive	miryokuteki(na)
audience	chōshū; shichōsha; chōshusha
auditor	chōkōsei; bōchōnin
auditorium	kōdō
August	hachigatsu
aunt	oba
author	chosha
authorized	seishiki ni ninkasareta
autobiography	jiden
automatic	(adj.) jidō(no)
automobile	jidōsha
autumn	aki
available	riyō dekiru; nyūshu-kanō(na)
average	(n.) heikin
	(adj.) heikin(no)
avoid	sakeru

await	matsu
awake	(v.) mezameru; okosu
award	(n.) shō
	(v.) (shō o) ataeru
aware	kizuiteiru
awful	hidoi
awfully	taihen
awkward	bukiyō(na); yakkai(na)
ax	(n.) ono
azalea	tsutsuji

3.

baby	(n.) akanbō
baby-sitter	komori
bachelor's degree	gakushigō
back	(n.) se; ushiro
	(adj.) ushiro(no)
	(adv.) ushiro e; ushiro ni
	(v.) kōtai suru; enjo suru
back and forth	zengo ni; ittari-kitari
backpack	(n.) ryukku-sakku
bacon	bēkon
bad	(adj.) warui; mazui
baggage	tenimotsu
baggage claim	tenimotsu-uketorijo
bake	(v.) yaku; yakeru
bakery	panya
balance	(n.) tsuriai; zandaka
bald	hageta
ball	tama; bōru
balloon	(n.) hūsen; kikyū
ballot	(n.) tōhyō-yōshi
bamboo	take
banana	banana
bandage	(n.) hōtai
	(v.) hōtai suru
bank	(n.) ginkō

bank book	ginkō-tsūchō
banquet	(n.) enkai
baptism	senrei
barbaric	soya(na)
barbecue	(n.) bābekyū
barber shop	rihatsuten; tokoya
bare	(adj.) hadaka(no)
barn	naya
base	(n.) kiso; kichi
baseball	yakyū
basement	chikai; chikashitsu
bashful	hanikamiya(no); uchiki(na)
basic	kiso(no)
basically	honshitsuteki ni
basket	kago; zaru
bath	nyūyoku; yokushitsu
bathing suit	mizugi
bathroom	yokushitsu; huroba
bean	mame
bear	(n.) kuma
bearable	gaman-dekiru
beard	(n.) hige
beat	(v.) tataku; uchimakasu
beautiful	utsukushii; subarashii
beauty mark	hokuro
beauty parlor	biyōin
because	...nanode
because of	...no tame ni
become	...ni naru
becoming	husawashii; niau
bed	(n.) beddo; nedoko
bed & breakfast	minshuku; ippaku-chōshoku-tsuki
bedroom	shinshitsu
bee	mitsubachi
beef	gyūniku
beer	bīru

before	(adv.) mae e; mae ni
	(prep.) ...no mae ni
	(conj.) ...suru mae ni
beforehand	(adv.) maemotte
beggar	(n.) kojiki
begin	hajimeru; hajimaru
beginner	shoshinsha
beginning	hajimari; hajime
Beg your pardon	Nan to osshaimashita ka?; Shitsurei-shimashita.
behave oneself	gyōgi o yokusuru
behavior	hurumai; taido
behind	(adv.) ushiro ni; okurete
	(prep.) ...no ato ni; ...ni okurete
belief	shin´nen; shinkō
believe	shinjiru; ...da to kangaeru
bell	(n.) suzu; kane
belong	...ni shozokusuru
belongings	shojihin; shoyūbutsu
beloved	(adj.) saiai(no); taisetsu(na)
	(n.) saiai no hito
below	(adv.) shita ni
	(prep.) ...no kahō ni
bend	(v.) mageru; magaru
benefactor	kōensha; kihusha
beneficial	yūeki(na)
benefit	(n.) rieki; onkei
benevolent	nasake-bukai; zen´i aru
benign	onwa(na); ryōsei(no)
bent	(adj.) magatta
beside	...no soba ni
besides	(prep.) ...no hoka ni
	(adv.) sono ue
best	(adj.) ichiban(no); kono ue nai
bet	(v.) kakeru; dangen suru
	(n.) kake
betray	uragiru

better	(adj.) yori yoi
	(adv.) issō yoku; sara ni yoku
between	(adv.) chūkan ni
	(prep.) ...no aida de; ...no aida ni
between you and me	kokodake no hanashidesu ga
beverage	nomimono
beware	yōjin suru
beyond	(prep.) ...no mukō ni; ...o koete; ...yori ijō ni
	(adv.) kanata ni
Bible	seisho
bibliography	sankō-shomoku
bicentennial	(n.) nihyakunen-me; nihyakunen-sai
bicycle	(n.) Jitensha
	(v.) jitensha ni noru
bid	(n.) nyūsatsu
big	(adj.) ookii
bilingal	nikakokugo o hanasu
bill	(n.) seikyūsho; shihei
billionaire	okuman-chōJa
bimonthly	(adj.) kakugetsu(no)
binoculars	sōgankyō
biography	denki
biology	seibutsugaku
biotechnology	idenshi-kōgaku; seibutsu-kōgaku
bird	tori
birds of a feather	onaji shumi no hito; dōgyōsha
bird´s-eye view	chōkanzu; gaikan
bird-watching	yachō-kansatsu
birth	tanjō; iegara
birth control	hinin
birthday	tanjōbi
bit	kakera; shōryō
bite	(v.) kamu; kajiru
	(n.) hitokuchi
bitter	(adj.) nigai; tsurai
biweekly	(adj.) kakushū(no)

	(adv.) kakushū ni
black	(adj.) kuroi
	(n.) kuro
black tea	kōcha
blame	(v.) hinan suru; togameru
	(n.) hinan
blank	(adj.) kūhaku(no)
	(n.) hakushi
blanket	(n.) mōfu
blasphemy	bōtoku
bleach	(v.) hyōhaku suru
bleeding	(n.) shukketsu
blend	(v.) mazeawaseru
blessed	megumareta; saiwai(na)
blind	(adj.) mōmoku(no)
	(n.) sudare; buraindo
blister	mizu-bukure; hi-bukure
blood	(n.) ketsueki
blood pressure	ketsuatsu
bloodshot	(me ga) jūketsu-shita
blood type	ketsueki-gata
bloom	(v.) hana ga saku
blossom	(n.) (kaju no) hana
blouse	(n.) burausu
blow	(v.) huku; kaze ga huku
blue	(adj.) aoi
	(n.) ao
blush	(v.) sekimen suru
board of education	kyōiku-iinkai
boast	(v.) jiman suru
boat	(n.) kobune; bōto; hune
body	(n.) karada
body language	miburi-gengo
boil	(v.) wakasu; waku; niru; nieru
bold	daitan(na)
bomb	(v.) bakugeki suru

	(n.) bakudan
bond	(n.) kizuna; saiken
bone	(n.) hone
book	(n.) hon; shomotsu
	(v.) (zaseki nado o) yoyaku suru
bookkeeping	boki
book review	shohyō
bookshelf	shodana
bookstore	honya
border	(n.) sakai; kokkyō
boring	taikutsu(na)
borough	gyōsei-ku; jichi-chōson
borrow	kariru
botanical garden	shokubutsuen
both	(adj.) ryōhō(no)
	(prop.) ryōhō
	(adv.) ryōhō tomo
bother	(v.) nayamasu; ki o momu
	(n.) mendō
bottle	(n.) bin
bottom	(n.) soko; kontei
bottom line	yōten; hon'ne; girigiri no tokoro
bracket	(n.) kakko
	(v.) kakko de kakomu
Braille	(n.) tenji
brain	(n.) nō; zunō; chiteki-shidōsha
brain death	nōshi
branch	(n.) eda
branch office	shiten; shisha
brand-new	maatarashii
brave	(adj.) yūkan(na)
bread	pan; shushoku
bread and butter	(n.) seikei; batā-tsuki pan
breadth	haba; hirosa
break	(v.) kowareru; kowasu; wareru; waru
breakable	(adj.) koware-yasui

breakfast	chōshoku; asa-gohan
breath	kokyū; iki
breathe	kokyū o suru
breeze	(n.) soyokaze
bribe	(n.) wairo
brick	(n.) renga
bride	hanayome; shinpu
bridegroom	hanamuko; shinrō
bridge	(n.) hashi
briefly	temijika ni; kantan ni
bright	(adj.) akarui; sōmei(na)
brilliant	kirakira-shita; rippa(na); atama no surudoi
bring	motte-kuru; tsurete-kuru
bring back	modosu; kaesu
bring out	mochidasu
bring up	sodateru
brisk	genki(na); kibikibi-shita
briskly	genki yoku
broad	(adj.) hirobiro to shita
broadcast	(v.) hōsō suru
broadcasting	hōsō
broad-minded	kokoro no hiroi
broccoli	burokkori
brochure	panhuretto
broken	kowareta; yabureta; hasan-shita
brokenhearted	shitsuren-shita; shōshin(no)
bronchitis	kikanshi-en
brook	ogawa
broom	(n.) hōki
brother	kyōdai
brown	(n.) chairo
	(adj.) chairo(no)
brown rice	genmai
bruise	(n.) dabokushō
brunch	chōshoku-ken-chūshoku; osoi chōshoku
brush up	migaki o kakeru; yarinaosu

bubble	(n.) awa
bucket	(n.) baketsu
bud	(n.) tsubomi; me
Buddhism	(n.) Bukkyō
budget	(n.) yosan; keihi
build	(v.) tateru; kizuku; tsukuru
building	tatemono
build-in	tsukuri-tsuke(no)
bulb	denkyū; kyūkon
bull	(n.) oushi
bulletin board	keijiban
bump	(v.) tsukiataru
bundle	(n.) tsutsumi; taba
bunk bed	nidan-beddo
burden	(n.) omoni; hutan
bureaucratic	oyakushoteki(na)
burglar	gōtō
burn	(v.) moyasu; moeru; yakedo o suru
	(n.) yakedo; hiyake
bus	(n.) basu
business	shigoto; yōken
business hour	eigyō-jikan; kinmu-jikan
businesslike	jimuteki(na)
business school	keieigaku-daigakuin
busy	(adj.) isogashii
but	(conj.) shikashi; keredomo
	(prep.) ...o nozoite wa
butcher	(n.) nikuya
butterfly	chō
button	(n.) botan
	(v.) botan o kakeru
buy	(v.) kau
	(n.) kaimono; horidashi-mono
by	(prep.) ...no soba ni; ...ni yotte; ...de
by and large	gaishite; zenpanteki ni mite
by oneself	dokuryoku de; hitori-bocchi de

by the way	tokoro de

C.

cab	takushī
cabbage	kyabetsu
Cabinet	Naikaku
cactus	saboten
cafe	kissaten
cake	(n) kēki
calculate	keisan suru; mitsumoru; suitei suru
calculating	dasanteki(na)
calculator	keisanki
calendar	koyomi; karendā
call	(v.) yobu; denwa o kakeru
calligraphy	shodō
calling card	meishi
calm	(adj.) heion(na); shizuka(na)
camel	rakuda
camera	kamera
campaign	(n.) yūzei; kyanpēn
campus	kōtei; kōnai
can	(aux. v.) ...dekiru; ...shite mo ii
canal	unga
cancel	(v.) torikesu
cancer	gan
candidate	kōhosha; shigansha
candle	rōsoku
candy	(n.) satō-gashi; ame
cane	(n.) tsue
canned goods	kanzume-rui
cannot	(aux. v.) ...dekinai; ...shite wa ikenai
can opener	kankiri
canyon	dai-kyōkoku
cap	bōshi
capability	nōryoku; sainō
capable	nōryoku no aru
capacity	(n.) shūyōryoku; rikiryō

cape	misaki
capital	(n.) shuto; shihon
capitalism	shihon-shugi
capital letter	ōmoji
car	kuruma
cardboard	danbōru; bōrugami
cardiac	(adj.) shinzō(no)
	(n.) shinzōbyō-kanja
cardinal number	kisū
care	(n.) shinpai; yōjin; sewa
care about	...o ki ni kakeru
care for	konomu
carefree	nonbiri-shita
careful	chūibukai; ki o tsukeru
carefully	chūibukaku
careless	huchūi(na); keisotsu(na)
caretaker	kanrinin
caricature	giga; hūshibun
carnation	kāneishon
carpenter	(n.) daiku
carrot	ninjin
carry	(v.) hakobu; motte-iku; shoji suru
cartoon	(n.) manga
carve	chōkoku suru
cascade	kotaki; wakare-daki
case	baai; jijō; jiken; jirei
cash	(n.) genkin
cash a check	kogitte o genkin ni kaeru
Cash or charge	genkin-barai desu ka, soretomo, kurejitto-kādo desu ka?
census	kokusei-chōsa
centennial	(n.) hyakunen-sai
center	(n.) chūshin; chūō
centigrade	sesshi-ondokei
central	(adj.) chūō(no)
centralize	chūō-shūkenka suru

century	seiki
ceramics	tōjiki-rui
ceremony	gishiki
certain	(adj.) tashika(na)
certainly	tashika ni; mochiron
certificate	(n.) shōmeisho; menkyojō
certify	shōmei suru; hoshō suru
chain	(n.) kusari
chair	(n.) isu
chairperson	gichō
challenge	(v.) chōsen suru
challenging	kyomi o sosoru; chōsenteki(na)
chance	(n.) kikai; un; mikomi
chancellor	(daigaku no) sōchō
change	(n.) henka; norikae; otsuri
	(v.) kaeru; kawaru
changeable	kaerareru; kawari-yasui
chaperon	tsukisoi
chapter	(shomotsu no) shō
character	seikaku; jinkaku; tokusei
characteristic	(n.) tokuchō
	(adj.) tokuyū(no)
charge	(v.) (ryōkin, daikin nado o) seikyū suru; tsuke ni suru
charity	jiai; jizen-jigyō
charm	(n.) miryoku; omamori
charming	miryokuteki(na)
chase	(n.) tsuiseki
	(v.) oikakeru
chat	(n.) zatsudan
	(v.) zatsudan o suru
cheap	(adj.) yasui; yasuppoi
cheat	(n.) gomakashi; kan'ningu
	(v.) gomakasu; azamuku
check	(n.) kogitte; kensa
checkbook	kogitte-chō

check-in	shukuhaku-tetsuzuki; tōjō-tetsuzuki
check in	chekku-in suru
checkup	kenkō-shindan
cheek	(n.) hoo
cheerful	hogaraka(na)
chemistry	kagaku
cherish	daiji ni suru; itsukushimu
cherry	(n.) sakura; sakuranbo
chest of drawers	tansu
chestnut	kuri
chew	(v.) yoku kamu
chicken	(n.) niwatori; keiniku
child	kodomo
child abuse	jidō-gyakutai
childhood	yōnenki
childlike	mujaki(na)
chill	(n.) kanki; samuke
chilly	hiebie suru
chimney	entotsu
chin	(n.) ago
chinaware	setomono
choir	gasshōdan; seikatai
choke	(v.) iki ga tsumaru
choose	erabu
chore	zatsuyō; kaji
christianity	kirisuto-kyō
chronologically	nendai-jun ni
church	kyōkai
cider	ringoshu
cinema	eiga
circulate	junkan suru; kairan saseru
circumstance	jijō; jōkyō
citizen	shimin; jūmin
citizenship	shiminken; kōminken
city	tokai; toshi
city hall	shiyakusho

civil engineering	doboku-kōgaku
civilization	bunmei
civilized	bunmeika sareta; reigi-tadashii
claim	(v.) yōkyū suru; shuchō suru
	(n.) yōkyū; shuchō
clam	hamaguri
clap	(v.) hakushu o suru
clarify	akiraka ni suru
clash	(n.) shōtotsu
	(v.) shōtotsu suru
class	(n.) gakkyū; jugyō; kaikyū
classic	(adj.) kotenteki(na); dentōteki(na)
	(n.) koten; meisaku
classroom	kyōshitsu
claw	(n.) tsume
clean	(adj.) seiketsu(na); keppaku(na)
	(adv.) kirei ni
	(v.) kirei ni suru
cleaner's	sentaku-ya
cleaning	sōji; sentaku
clear	(adj.) sunda; hareta
clearly	hakkiri
clerk	jimuin; ten'in
clever	kashikoi; rikō(na)
client	irainin; kokyaku
cliff	gake
climate	kikō; fūdo
climb	(v.) noboru
clinic	shinryōjo
clinical thermometer	taionkei
clock	tokei
clockwise	(adv.) migimawari ni
close	(v.) tojiru; shimeru
	(adj.) tojita; shinmitsu(na); chikai
closet	(n.) oshiire; todana
cloth	nuno

clothes	ihuku
clothing	irui
cloud	(n.) kumo
cloudy	kumotta; nigotta
clumsy	bukiyō(na); bukakkō(na)
coal	(n.) sekitan
coarse	sozatsu(na); kime no arai
coast	(n.) kaigan
coat	(n.) uwagi; gaitō
coeducation	danjo-kyōgaku
coexist	kyōzon suru
cogitate	hukaku kangaeru
cognitive	ninshikiryoku no aru
cohabit	dōsei suru
coherent	shubiikkan-shita
coin	(n.) kōka; kozeni
coincidence	icchi
cold	(adj.) samui; tsumetai
	(n.) kanbō; kaze
collaborate	kyōryoku suru; kyōdō-kenkyū suru
collar	(n.) eri
colleague	dōryō
collect	(v.) atsumeru; atsumaru
collect call	ryōkin jushin'nin-barai tsūwa
college	daigaku; senmon-gakkō
collision	shōtotsu; huwa
colloquial	kōgotai(no); kaiwatai(no)
colonial	(adj.) shokuminchi(no)
color	(n.) iro; shikisai
	(v.) someru; irozuku
colorful	hanayaka(na)
comb	(n.) kushi
combine	(v.) ketsugō suru; rengō suru
	(n.) kigyō-gōdō
come	kuru; (aite no tokoro e) iku
come about	okoru

come across	deau
come back	modotte-kuru
come down	orite-kuru
come in	hairu
come up with	oitsuku
comedy	kigeki
comfort	(v.) nagusameru
	(n.) nagusame
comfortable	kokochi yoi
comical	kokkei (na)
command	(v.) meirei suru; (kotoba o) jiyu ni ayatsuru
	(n.) meirei; kushi-nōryoku
commemorate	iwau; kinen suru
commencement	sotsugyō-shiki
commercialize	shōgyōka suru
committee	iinkai
commodity	shōhin; nichiyōhin
common	(adj.) kyōtsū (no); hutsū (no)
common sense	jōshiki
common wealth	renpō; kyōwakoku
communicate	tsutaeru
communication	dentatsu; renraku
communism	kyōsan-shugi
community	kyōdō-shakai; kyōdōtai
commute	(v.) tsūkin suru
company	kōsai; nakama; kaisha
comparatively	hikakuteki ni
compare	(v.) hikaku suru
compatible	tekigō suru
compel	kyōyō suru
compete	kyōsō suru
competent	yūnō (na); tekitō (na)
competetion	kyōsō
complain	(v.) huhei o iu
	(n.) huhei; kujō
complete	(v.) kanzen ni suru; kansei suru

	(adj.) kanzen(na)
completely	kanzen ni
complicated	hukuzatsu(na)
composition	sakubun; sakkyoku
comprehend	rikai suru
comprehensible	rikai-dekiru; wakari-yasui
compromise	(n.) dakyō
	(v.) dakyō suru
compulsory education	gimu-kyōiku
concentrate	(v.) shūchū suru
conception	gainen
concern	(v.) kenen suru; ...ni kankei suru
	(n.) shinpai; kigakari; kankei
concerning	(prep.) ...ni kanshite
concise	kanketsu(na)
conclude	ketsuron suru; suidan suru
conclusion	ketsumatsu; ketsuron
condition	(n.) jōtai; jōkyō; jōken
conditional	jōkenzuki(no); kateiteki(na)
condominium	(bunjō-shiki) manshon
conductor	an'naisha; shikisha
confectionery	kashirui; kashiten
conference	kaigi
confess	uchiakeru
confidence	jishin; himitsu
confident	jishin no aru; kakushin no aru
confidential	naimitsu(no)
confirm	kakunin suru
confirmation	kakunin
confused	towaku shite
confusing	towaku-saseru
congratulate	shuku suru; omedetō to iu
Congressman	kain-giin
connection	renraku; setsuzoku; kankei
conquer	seihuku suru; kokuhuku suru
conscience	ryōshin; dōtokushin

consent	(v.) shōdaku suru; dōi suru
	(n.) shōdaku; dōi
consequently	shitagatte
conservative	(adj.) hoshuteki(na)
consider	kōryo suru
considerably	sōtō ni; kanari
considerate	omoiyari no aru
consideration	kōryo; omoiyari
consist of	...kara naru
consistent	shubi-ikkan shita
constantly	taezu
constitution	kenpō; kōsei; taishitsu
construct	(v.) kenzō suru
constructive	kensetsuteki(na)
consulate	ryōjikan
consult	sōdan suru
consume	shōhi suru
consumer	shōhisha
contact	(v.) renraku suru
contain	hukumu
contaminate	osen suru
contemporary	(adj.) gendai(no); saishinshiki(no)
content	(n.) naiyō; mokuji
	(adj.) manzoku-shite
continent	(n.) tairiku; hondo
contingent	(adj.) gūhatsuteki(na)
continually	taezu
continue	tsuzukeru; tsuzuku
continuing education	seijin-kyōiku
contract	(v.) keiyaku suru
	(n.) keiyaku
contradictory	mujunshita
contrarily	hantai ni
contrast	(n.) taishō; taihi
contribute	kōken suru; kihu suru; kikō suru
control	(v.) shihai suru; kanri suru

controversy	ronsō
convenient	benri(na)
conventional	kanshūteki(na)
conversation	kaiwa
converse	(v.) danwa suru
convey	dentatsu suru; hakobu
convince	nattoku saseru
cook	(v.) ryōri suru
	(n.) ryōrinin
cool	(adj.) suzushii
cooperate	kyōryoku suru
cope	(v.) umaku taisho suru
copper	(n.) dō
copyright	chosakuken
cordial	kokoro kara no
corn	tōmorokoshi
corporation	hōjin; kabushiki-gaisha
correct	(adj.) tadashii
	(v.) teisei suru; naosu
correctly	seikaku ni
correspond	hugō suru; buntsū suru
cosmetic	(n.) keshōhin
cosmopolitan	(adj.) kokusaiteki(na)
	(n.) kokusaijin
cost	(n.) hiyō; kakaku
co-star	(n.) kyōensha
cost of living	seikatsuhi
cotton	(n.) momen
couch	(n.) nagaisu; neisu
cough	(n.) seki
	(v.) seki o suru
counsellor	komon; sōdan-aite
count	kazoeru
countenance	(n.) kaotsuki; yōbō
count on	...o ate ni suru
country	(n.) kuni; inaka; kokyō

courage	yūki
courageous	yūkan (na)
courtesy	reigi; kōi
courthouse	saibansho
cousin	itoko
cove	irie
cover	(v.) oou; tsutsumu
cover charge	sābisu-ryō
cow	nyūgyū
coward	(adj.) okubyō (na)
cozy	igokochi no yoi
crab	(n.) kani
cracked	wareta
craftsman	shokunin; meikō
cramp	(n.) keiren
crane	(n.) tsuru
crash	(v.) shōtotsu suru; tsuiraku suru
crawl	(v.) hau; noronoro ugoku
crazy for	muchū (na)
cream puff	shū-kurīmu
creative	sōzōteki (na); sōsakuteki (na)
creature	ikimono
credibility	shinpyōsei; kakujitsusei
credit card	kurejitto-kādo
creek	ogawa
crescent	(n.) mikazuki
crime	hanzai
crisis	kiki; nankyoku
critical	hihanteki (na); jūdai (na)
critically	hihanteki ni
crooked	magatta; yuganda
crop	(n.) sakumotsu
cross	(v.) wataru; yokogiru
crossing	kōsaten
crosswalk	ōdan-hodō
crow	karasu

crowded	komiatta
crown prince	kōtaishi
crown princess	kōtaishi-hi
crucial	jūdai(na); kibishii
cry	(v.) sakebu
	(n.) sakebi-goe; nakigoe
crystallize	meikaku ni suru; gutaika suru
cultivate	tagayasu; migaku
culture	(n.) kyōyō; bunka
cure	(v.) chiryō suru; naosu
	(n.) chiryō; kyusai
curiosity	kōkishin; kottōhin
curious	mezurashii; kōkishin no tsuyoi
curriculum vitae	rirekisho
curry and rice	karē-raisu
curtain	kāten; maku
curve	(v.) mageru; magaru
custodian	kanrinin; hogosha
custom	(n.) shūkan; fūshū
customary	kanshūteki(na)
customer	kokyaku; tokuisaki
customhouse	zeikan
custom-made	atsurae(no)
cut	(v.) kiru
cut down	sakugen suru
cut in	warikomu; kanshō suru
cute	kawaii
cynical	hiniku(na)

D.	**daffodil**	rappa-zuisen
	daily	(adj.) mainichi(no)
		(adv.) hibi; higoto ni
	dainty	(adj.) jōhin(na)
	dairy farm	rakunōjō
	dairy products	nyūseihin
	damage	(n.) songai; sonshō

	(v.) kizutsukeru
damp	(adj.) shimeppoi
dance	(n.) odori
	(v.) odoru
dandelion	tanpopo
dangerous	kiken(na)
dare	(v.) omoikitte...suru
dark	(adj.) kurai
data	shiryō
date	(n.) hizuke; dēto
	(v.) dēto o suru
date line	hizuke-henkōsen
daughter	musume
daughter-in-law	musuko no tsuma
dawn	(n.) yoake
day	hi
day after day	hibi
day in and day out	aketemo kuretemo
day-care center	hoikusho
daylight saving time	natsu-jikan
daytime	hiruma
dead	(adj.) shinda
dead end	yukidomari
deadline	saishū-kigen
deaf	mimi ga kikoenai
deal	(v.) atsukau; torihiki o suru
dean	gakubuchō
dear	(adj.) shin'ai(na); itoshii
	(n.) kawaii-hito
Dear, dear	Oya, oya.
death	shi
debate	(v.) tōron suru
	(n.) tōron
debt	husai; ongi
decade	jūnen
decay	(v.) kusaru; otoroeru

decayed tooth	mushiba
deceive	damasu
decent	jōhin(na)
decide	kimeru
declare	sengen suru; genmei suru
decline	(v.) katamuku; teika suru
decrease	(v.) genshō suru; genshō saseru
dedicate	sasageru
deed	kōi
deep-rooted	nebukai
deer	shika
defeat	(v.) makasu
	(n.) haiboku
defect	(n.) kekkan; ketten
deficiency	husoku; kekkan
definition	teigi
defy	(v.) idomu; hankō suru
degree	teido; do
delay	(v.) okuraseru
	(n.) chien; enki
delegation	daihyōdan
delete	sakujo suru
deliberate	(adj.) koi(no)
deliberately	koi ni
delicate	binkan(na); sensai(na)
delicious	oishii
delighted	tanoshii; ureshii
delightful	tanoshii; ureshii
deliver	haitatsu suru; tsutaeru
delivery	haitatsu; hanashiburi
delivery man	haitatsu-nin
demand	(n.) yōkyū
	(v.) yōkyū suru
demeanor	taido
demerit	ketten
demilitarize	hibusōka suru

democracy	minshushugi
democratic	minshuteki (na)
demolish	hakai suru
demonstrative	jisshōteki (na)
den	ana; su; shigoto-beya
dense	misshūshita
density	mitsudo; nōdo
dentist	shikai; haisha
deny	hitei suru; kobamu
depart	shuppatsu suru
department	bu; shō; kyoku; ka
department store	depāto; hyakkaten
departure	shuppatsu
depend	tayoru
dependent	(adj.) tayotte
	(n.) huyō-kazoku
depict	byōsha suru
deposit	(v.) azukeru
depressed	hukeiki (na)
depressing	yuutsu (na)
depth	hukasa
deputy	dairinin; shisetsu
descend	kudaru; oriru
descendant	shison
describe	kijutsu suru; byōsha suru
description	byōsha; setsumei
desert	(n.) sabaku
deserve	...ni atai suru
designate	(v.) ninmei suru; meiji suru
desirable	konomashii
desire	(n.) ganbō; yokkyū
	(v.) negau; nozomu
desk	(n.) tsukue
desperate	zetsubōteki (na)
desperately	hisshi ni
dessert	dezāto

destination	ikisaki; mokutekichi
destiny	unmei
destitute	hinkon (no)
destroy	horobosu
destructive	hakaiteki (na)
detailed	shōsai (na)
detective	(n.) keiji; tantei
detergent	(n.) senzai
deteriorate	akka suru
determine	kesshin suru
determined	danko to shite
detour	(n.) mawari-michi
develop	hatten saseru; tenkai suru
development	hattatsu; hatten
device	sōchi; kuhū
devoted	kenshinteki (na)
dew	tsuyu; shizuku
diabetes	tōnyōbyō
diagnosis	shindan
diagonal	naname (no)
dialect	hōgen; namari
diameter	chokkei
diaper	omutsu
diary	nikki
dictionary	jisho; jiten
die	(v.) shinu
diet	(n.) shokuji-ryōhō; daietto
Diet	gikai; kokkai
difference	sōi; sai
different	kotonatta; betsu (no)
difficult	muzukashii
dig	(v.) horu
digest	(v.) shōka suru; nattoku suru
dignified	igen no aru; hin'i no aru
dignity	igen; songen
diligent	kinben (na)

dining car	shokudōsha
dining room	shokudō
dinner	yūshoku; seisan
diploma	sotsugyō-shōsho
diplomat	gaikōkan
diplomatic	gaikōteki (na)
direct	(v.) shidō suru; kantoku suru
	(adj.) massugu (no); socchoku (na)
directory	(n.) jūshoroku; jinmeibo
dirty	(adj.) huketsu (na); yogoreta
disabled person	shōgaisha
disadvantage	huri
disagree	icchi shinai; iken ga awanai
disagreeable	huyukai (na)
disappear	mienaku naru
disappointed	shitsubō shita
disappointing	kitai-hazure (no)
disapprove	ninka shinai; sansei shinai
disaster	saigai; sainan
discard	(v.) suteru
discipline	(n.) kunren; kiritsu
disclose	happyō suru; uchiakeru
discontinue	chūshi suru
discount	(n.) waribiki
	(v.) waribiki suru
discover	mitsukeru
discriminate	kubetsu suru
discrimination	sabetsu; kubetsu
discuss	rongi suru
discussion	tōron
disgraceful	hazukashii; humeiyo (na)
disguise	(v.) hensō suru; itsuwaru
	(n.) hensō; misekake
disgusting	mukatsukuyō (na)
dish	(n.) sara; ryōri
dishonor	humeiyo

dish towel	hukin
dishwasher	sara-araiki
disinfect	shōdoku suru
dislike	(v.) kirau
dismiss	kaisan saseru; kaiko suru
disorder	(n.) konran; byōki
dispatch	(n.) kyūso; hassō
display	(v.) tenji suru; hirogeru
	(n.) tenji; koji
disposable	(adj.) tsukai-sute(no)
disposition	seishitsu; kidate
dispute	(v.) giron suru
disqualified	shikaku no nai
dissatisfaction	human; huhei
dissect	(v.) kaibō suru
dissimilar	niteinai
distance	(n.) kyori
distant	tōi
distinguish	kubetsu suru
distortion	yugami; waikyoku
distribute	bunpai suru; hirogeru
district	chiku; chihō
disturb	samatageru; jama suru
diversity	sōi; tayōsei
divide	(v.) wakeru; wakareru
divorce	(n.) rikon
	(v.) rikon suru
dizzy	(adj.) memai no suru
do	suru; okonau
doctor	(n.) ishi; hakase
doctorate	hakasegō
document	(n.) shorui
dog	(n.) inu
doggie bag	tabenokoshi o mochikaeru kamibukuro
doll	ningyō
dollar	doru

domestic	(adj.) kateinai (no); kokunai (no)
donation	kihu
door	to; tobira
dormitory	ryō; kishikusha
dose	(n.) (kusuri no) ippuku
dot	(n.) ten
	(v.) ten o utsu
double	(adj.) nibai (no); nijū (no)
doubt	(v.) utagau
	(n.) utagai
doubtful	utagawashii
dove	hato
down	(prep.) ...o kudatte; shita ni
	(adv.) shita e; shita ni
down payment	atamakin
downstairs	(adv.) kaika ni
downtown	(adj.) hankagai (no)
	(adv.) hankagai ni
doze	(v.) inemuri suru
	(n.) inemuri
dozen	dāsu; jūni
dragonfly	tonbo
drama	shibai; engeki
draw	(v.) hiku; hikiyoseru
dream	(n.) yume
	(v.) yume o miru
dress	(n.) ihuku; hukusō
	(v.) ihuku o kiru; ihuku o kiseru
dress up	kikazaru
dressing table	keshōdai
drink	(v.) nomu
	(n.) nomimono; sake
drive	(v.) karitateru; unten suru
driver	untenshu
driver´s license	unten-menkyosho
drop by	chotto tachiyoru

drop out	rakugo suru; chūto-taigaku suru
drunken	yotta
dry	(adj.) kawaita
	(v.) kawaku; kawakasu
duck	kamo; ahiru
due to	...no tame; shiharai-kijitsu no kita
duplicate	(n.) utsushi; mozōhin
during	...no aida; ...jū
dust	(n.) hokori; chiri
Dutch treat	warikan
duty	gimu; shokumu; shigoto
duty-free	menzei(no)
dwell	sumu
dye	someru; somaru

E. each	(adj.) sore-zore(no)
	(pron.) kakuji; sore-zore
each other	otagai ni
eager	shikiri ni...shitagatte; nesshin(na)
eagerly	nesshin ni
ear	mimi
early	(adj.) hayai
	(adv.) hayaku; osanai koro ni
earn	kasegu
earnest	(adj.) majime(na); nesshin(na)
earth	(n.) daichi; jimen; chikyū
earthquake	jishin
easily	yōi ni; rakuraku to
east	(n.) higashi
eastern	(adj.) tōbu(no)
easy	(adj.) yasashii; kiraku(na)
easygoing	nonki(na)
eat	(v.) taberu
echo	(n.) kodama; hankyō
ecology	seitai-kankyō; seitaigaku
economical	keizaiteki(na)

economics	keizaigaku
edit	henshū suru
educate	kyōiku suru
educated	kyōyō no aru
education	kyōiku
educator	kyōikusha
eel	unagi
effect	(n.) kekka; eikyō
effective	(adj.) yūko(na); kōkateki(na)
efficient	yūno(na); nōritsuteki(na)
effort	doryoku
egg	tamago
egoistic	rikoteki(na); wagamama(na)
egotistical	jiko-chūshin(no)
eight	(n.) hachi
eighteen	(n.) jū-hachi
eighth	(n.) dai-hachi
eighty	(n.) hachijū
either	(adj.) dochiraka(no)
	(pron.) dochiraka
elaborate	(adj.) seikō(na); kotta
elbow	(n.) hiji
elder	(adj.) toshiue(no)
elderly	(adj.) shorō(no)
elect	(v.) erabu
election	senkyo
elective subject	sentaku-kamoku
electricity	denki
electronics	denshi-kōgaku
elegant	yūga(na); jōhin(na)
elementary school	shōgakkō
elephant	zō
eleven	(n.) jū-ichi
eleventh	(n.) dai-jūichi
eligible	(adj.) tekikaku(na)
eliminate	(v.) sakujo suru

eloquent	yūben (na)
else	hoka ni; sono hoka
embarrassing	komatta; yakkai (na)
embassy	taishikan
embrace	(v.) dakishimeru
emerge	ukabideru; arawareru
emergency	hijō-jitai
emergency exit	hijō-guchi
emigration	ijū; imin
eminent	chomei (na); sugureta
emotional	kanjōteki (na)
emperor	ten'nō
emphasize	kyōchō suru
employ	(v.) koyō suru; shiyō suru
employee	jūgyōin
employer	koyō-nushi
employment	koyō; shigoto
empress	kōgō
empty	(adj.) kara (no); munashii
enable	kanō ni suru
enclose	dōhū suru; kakomu
encounter	(v.) deau
	(n.) sōgu
encourage	yūkizukeru
encouragement	gekirei
end	(n.) owari
endeavor	(v.) doryoku suru
	(n.) doryoku
endorse	uragaki suru; hoshō suru
endure	taeru
energetic	seiryokuteki (na)
energy	katsudōryoku; enerugī
engagement	yakusoku; yōji; konyaku
engineering	kōgaku
English	(n.) eigo; eikokujin
	(adj.) eigo (no); eikoku (no)

engrave	chōkoku suru
enhance	takameru; masu
enjoy	tanoshimu
enjoyment	tanoshimi
enlargement	kakudai; zōdai
enough	(adj.) jūbun(na)
	(adv.) jūbun ni
enter	hairu
entertain	motenasu; tanoshimaseru
enthusiastic	nesshin(na)
entire	(adj.) zentai(no)
entirely	mattaku
entrance	iriguchi
entrance examination	nyūgaku-shiken
entrance fee	nyūjōryō; nyūgakukin
envelope	hūtō
environment	kankyō
environmental pollution	kankyō-osen; kōgai
envy	(v.) urayamu
epidemic	(adj.) ryūkosei(no)
equal	(adj.) hitoshii
equality	byōdō
equal opportunity	(koyō ni okeru) kikai-kintō
equipment	sōbi; setsubi
equivalent	(adj.) dōtō(no); hitoshii
erase	kesu
eraser	kesu-mono
errand	yōji; tsukai
error	machigai
eruption	hunka; bakuhatsu
escalator	esukarētā
escape	(v.) nigeru
especially	toku ni
essay	(n.) shōron; zuihitsu
essential	(adj.) honshitsuteki(na); hukaketsu(no)
establish	(v.) setsuritsu suru; kakuritsu suru

estate	zaisan; hudōsan-ken
estimate	(v.) mitsumoru
eternally	eien ni
ethnic	jinshu(no); minzoku(no)
etiquette	sahō
European	(adj.) ōshū(no); ōshūjin(no)
	(n.) ōshūjin
evaluate	(v.) hyōka suru
even	(adj.) taira(na); kōhei(na)
	(adv.) ...de sae mo; nao issō
evening	yūgata; ban
event	dekigoto; gyōji
eventually	kekkyoku wa; tsui ni
everybody	daredemo; mina
everything	nanimo kamo
everywhere	doko demo
evidence	shōko; shōgen
exactly	seikaku ni; masa ni
exaggeration	kochō
examine	shiken suru; kensa suru
example	(n.) rei; jitsurei
exceedingly	hijō ni
excellent	(adj.) yūshū(na); batsugun(no)
except	(prep.) ...o nozoite wa
exception	reigai
exceptional	reigaiteki(na)
excessive	kado(no); kyokutan(na)
exchange	(v.) kōkan suru
	(n.) kōkan; ryōgae
exciting	shigekiteki(na); hijō ni omoshiroi
exclusive	(adj.) haitateki(na)
excuse	(v.) kanben suru; benkai suru
Excuse me	sumimasen.
exemption	menjo
exercise	(n.) renshū; undō; jikkō
exhaust	(v.) shōmō suru; tsukare saseru

exhibition	tenrankai; hakurankai
exist	sonzai suru
exit	deguchi
exotic	ikokuhū(no)
expand	(v.) hirogeru; hirogaru
expect	kitai suru; yoki suru
expedition	tanken
expense	hiyō; shuppi
expensive	kōka(na)
experience	(v.) keiken suru
	(n.) keiken
experimental	jikkenteki(na)
expert	(n.) senmonka
expire	kigen ga kireru; manki ni naru
explain	setsumei suru
explode	bakuhatsu suru; bakuhatsu saseru
explore	tanken suru
export	(v.) yushutsu suru
	(n.) yushutsu
express	(v.) hyōgen suru
	(adv.) kyūkō de; sokutatsu de
expressway	kosoku-dōro
exquisite	zetsumyō(na); seikō(na)
extend	nobasu; nobiru
exterior	(n.) gaibu; gaikan
extinguisher	shōkaki
extra	(adj.) yobun(na); tokubetsu(no)
	(adv.) yobun ni; tokubetsu ni
extraordinary	hibon(na); namihazureta
extravagant	(adj.) zeitaku(na)
extremely	hijō ni
eye	me
eyeglasses	megane
eyesight	shiryoku
F. fabric	orimono

fabulous	subarashii
face	(n.) kao
	(v.) ...ni men suru; tachimukau
facility	setsubi
fact	jijitsu
factory	kōjō
fade	(v.) shibomu; aseru
fail	(v.) shippai suru
failure	shippai; rakugosha
faint	(v.) ki o ushinau
fair	(adj.) kōsei(na); hareta; iro-jiro(no)
fairy tale	otogi-banashi
faith	shinkō; shin'nen
faithful	seijitsu(na)
fake	(n.) nisemono
	(adj.) nise(no)
fall	(v.) ochiru; taoreru; huru
false	(adj.) machigatta; nise(no)
familiar	(adj.) shitashii; yoku shitte-iru
family	kazoku
family name	sei; myōji
family tree	kakeizu
famous	yūmei(na)
fantastic	gensoteki(na); subarashii
far	(adj.) tōi
	(adv.) haruka ni
fare	(n.) ryōkin
farewell party	sōbetsukai
farm	(n.) nōjō
far-sighted	enshi(no)
fascinating	miwakuteki(na)
fashionable	(adj.) ryūkō(no)
fast	(adj.) hayai
	(adv.) hayaku
fasten	shikkari tomeru
fat	(n.) shibō

	(adj.) hutotta
fate	unmei
father	(n.) chichi; otōsan; shinpu
father-in-law	gihu
fatigue	(n.) hirō
fault	(n.) ketten; kashitsu
favor	(n.) kōi; shinsetsu; negai
favorable	kōiteki(na)
favorite	(adj.) ki ni iri(no)
fearful	kowai
feast	(n.) shukusai-jitsu; gochisō
feather	(n.) hane
feature	(n.) yōbō; tokushoku
February	nigatsu
federal	renpō(no); gasshū-koku(no)
fee	(n.) ryōkin; jugyōryō
feed	(v.) shokumotsu o ataeru
feel	(v.) hureru; kanjiru; ki ga suru
feeling	(n.) kanji; kanjō
fellow	(n.) nakama; dōryō; hito
female	(n.) josei
	(adj.) josei(no)
feminine	josei(no); on'narashii
fence	(n.) kakoi; saku
fertile	hiyoku(na); yutaka(na)
fertilizer	kagaku-hiryō
festival	(n.) matsuri; shukuen
fever	(n.) netsu
few	(adj.) wazuka(na)
fib	tawainai uso
fiber	sen'i-shitsu
field	(n.) nohara; hatake
fifteen	(n.) jū-go
fifty	(n.) go-jū
fifty-fifty	(adj.) gobu-gobu(no)
fight	(v.) tatakau

	(n.) tatakai
figure	(n.) katachi; sūji
	(v.) ...to omou; keisan suru
figure out	kangae-dasu; rikai suru
fill	(v.) mitasu; michiru
fill in	husagu; kaki-ireru
fill out	kakikomu
finally	saishūteki ni; tsui ni
financial	zaiseiteki(na)
find	(v.) mitsukeru
fine	(n.) bakkin
	(adj.) sugureta; rippa(na); hareta; komakai
fine arts	bijutsu
finger	(n.) yubi
fingerprint	(n.) shimon
finish	(v.) owaru; oeru
fire	(n.) hi; kaji
fire escape	hijō-kaidan
fire station	shōbōsho
firm	(adj.) kengo(na); shikkarishita
first	(n.) dai-ichibanme
	(adj.) saisho(no); saikō(no)
	(adv.) saisho ni
fiscal year	kaikei-nendo
fish	(n.) sakana
	(v.) tsuri o suru
fishing	sakana-tsuri
fit	(v.) au; awaseru
five	(n.) go
fix	(v.) shūri suru; yōi suru
flag	(n.) hata
flame	(n.) honoo
flashlight	kaichū-dentō
flat	(adj.) taira(na); tanchō(na)
flatter	oseji o iu
flea market	nomi-no-ichi

flexible	jūnan(na); yūzū no kiku
flight	hikōki no bin
flight attendant	kyakushitsu-jōmuin
float	(v.) uku; ukaseru
flood	(n.) kōzui
	(v.) hanran suru; ahureru
floor	(n.) yuka; kai
flour	komugi-ko
flower	(n.) hana
fluently	ryūchō ni
fly	(v.) tobu
focus	(n.) shōten
	(v.) shōten o awaseru
fog	(n.) kiri
fold	(v.) oritatamu
folk	(n.) hitobito
follow	(v.) tsuite-iku; shitagau
following	(adj.) tsugi(no)
fond	...ga suki de
food	tabemono
foolish	oroka(na); bakageta
foot	(n.) ashi; humoto
for	(prep.) ...no tame ni; ...no kawari ni
forbid	(v.) kinjiru
force	(n.) chikara
	(v.) kyōyō suru
forehead	hitai
foreign	gaikoku(no)
foreigner	gaikokujin
foreign exchange	gaikoku-kawase
forest	(n.) mori; hayashi
forever	eikyū ni
forget	wasureru
forgive	yurusu
formally	seishiki ni; keishikiteki ni
former	(adj.) mae(no); izen(no)

fortunate	kōun(na)
forty	(n.) yon-jū
forward	(v.) sokushin suru; tensō suru
foster	yōiku suru
found	sōritsu suru
foundation	kiso; zaidan
four	(n.) yon; shi
fourteen	(n.) jū-yon; jū-shi
fox	(n.) kitsune
fragile	koware-yasui
fragrance	kaguwashii kaori
frail	(adj.) moroi
frank	(adj.) socchoku(na)
free	(adj.) jiyū(na)
	(adv.) jiyū ni; muryō de
freedom	jiyū
freeze	(v.) kōru; kōraseru
frequently	tabitabi
fresh	(adj.) atarashii; shinsen(na); sawayaka(na)
freshman	(daigaku no) ichinensei; shin'nyūsei
Friday	kinyōbi
friend	(n.) tomodachi
friendly	shinsetsu(na); shitashimi-yasui
frighten	kowagaraseru
frog	kaeru
from	...kara
front	(n.) zenmen; shōmen
frost	(n.) shimo
frostbite	tōshō; shimoyake
frozen	kōtta; reitō(no)
frozen food	reitō-shokuhin
fruit	(n.) kudamono
fruitful	minori no ooi
frustration	yokkyū-human
fuel	nenryō
fulfill	hatasu; tassei suru

full	(adj.) ippai(no); yutaka(na)
full-time	jōkin(no); sen'nin(no)
fully	jūbun ni
fun	(n.) tanoshimi; yorokobi
fund	(n.) kikin; shikin
fundamental	(adj.) konponteki(na); shuyō(na)
funeral	(n.) sōshiki
funny	(adj.) kokkei(na); hen(na)
fur	kegawa
furniture	kagu
future	(adj.) shōrai(no)
	(n.) shōrai; kongo

G. gaily	yōki ni; hanayaka ni
gain	(v.) eru
galaxy	ginga
gallery	garō; bijutsukan
gamble	(v.) kakeru
	(n.) bakuchi
game	(n.) shōbu; kyōgi; tanoshimi
garage	(n.) shako; jidōsha shūri-kōjō
garbage	(n.) (daidokoro no) gomi
garden	(n.) niwa; saien
garden party	enyūkai
garlic	nin'niku
garment	ihuku
gas	(n.) gasorin; gasu
gate	(n.) mon; kaisatsu-guchi
gather	(v.) atsumeru; atsumaru
gay	(adj.) yōki(na); hade(na)
gaze	(v.) mitsumeru
gem	(n.) hōseki
gender	seibetsu; sei
gene	idenshi
general	(adj.) zenpanteki(na); hutsū(no)
generally speaking	ippanteki ni ieba

generation	sedai; shison
generous	kandai(na)
genius	tensai
gentle	onwa(na); yasashii
genuine	shinjitsu(no); honmono(no)
geography	chiri; chikei
geology	chishitsu; chishitsugaku
germ	saikin; byōgenkin
gesture	miburi
get	te ni ireru; tassuru; ...ni naru
get along with	...to umaku yaru
get off	oriru
get on	noru
get to	tōchaku suru
get up	okiru
gift	(n.) okurimono; tenpu no sai
gigantic	kyōdai(na)
ginger	shōga
girl	shōjo; on´na no ko
give	ataeru
give back	kaesu
give up	akirameru
glad	ureshii; ureshisō(na)
glance	(v.) chirari to miru
	(n.) ichibetsu
glasses	megane
global	sekaiteki(na)
glorious	haearu
glory	(n.) eikō; meiyo
glossary	(senmongo, tokushugo no) shō-jiten
glove	(n.) tebukuro
glue	(n.) nori; secchakuzai
go	iku; nakunaru
go by	tōrisugiru
go on	susumu; tsuzuku; tsuzukeru
go out	gaishutsu suru

goat	yagi
god	kami
God knows	Darenimo wakaranai.
gold	kin
golf	goruhu
good	yoi; tanoshii; oishii
Good afternoon	Kon'nichiwa.
Good-bye	Sayōnara.
Good evening	Konbanwa.
Good morning	Ohayō-gozaimasu.
Good night	Oyasumi-nasai.
gorgeous	subarashii; gōka(na)
Gospel	hukuinsho
gossip	(n.) uwasa-banashi; zatsudan
gourmet	shokutsū
Government	seihu; gyōsei
grab	(v.) hittsukamu
graceful	jōhin(na)
gracious	yūga(na); jōhin(na)
grade	(n.) tōkyū; hyōten; gakunen-kyū
grade school	shōgakkō
gradually	shidai ni
graduate	(v.) sotsugyō suru
	(n.) sotsugyō-sei
graduate school	daigakuin
graffiti	rakugaki
grammar	bunpō
grandchild	mago
grandfather	sohu
grandmother	sobo
grant	(n.) joseikin; hojokin
grape	budō
grapefruit	gurēpu-hurūtsu
grasp	(v.) nigiru; rikai suru
grass	(n.) shibahu; kusa
grassroots	konpon; taishū

grate	orosu; suritsubusu
grateful	(adj.) kansha suru; arigataku omou
gratitude	kansha
grave	(n.) haka
	(adj.) jūdai(na); genshuku(na)
gravity	inryoku
gray	(adj.) haiiro(no)
	(n.) haiiro
great	(adj.) jūyo(na); subrashii; okii
greedy	yoku-bukai
green	(adj.) midoriiro(no)
	(n.) midoriiro
green card	eijū-kyokashō
green tea	ryokucha; nihoncha
greeting	aisatsu
grief	kanashimi
grill	(v.) yaku; aburu
grind	(v.) suri-kudaku; kezuru
grocery	shokuryōhin-ten
ground	(n.) jimen; undōjō; konkyo
grow	sodatsu; ...ni naru
guarantee	(v.) hoshō suru
guess	(n.) suisoku
	(v.) suisoku suru
guest	kyaku
guide	(v.) an'nai suru; shidō suru
guilty	yūzai(no)
gulp	(v.) nomikomu
gymnastics	taisō; taiiku
gynecologist	hujinka-i

H.	habit	(n.) kuse; shūkan
	habitant	jūnin
	habitual	shūkanteki(na); jōshūteki(na)
	hail	(n.) hyō; arare
	hair	ke

half	(n.) hanbun
	(adj.) hanbun(no)
half-and-half	(adj.) hanhan(no)
ham	hamu
hand	te
Hands off	Hurete wa ikemasen.
Hand up	Te o agero.
handbill	chirashi; bira
handicapped	(shintaiteki aruiwa seishinteki ni) shōgai no aru
handmade	tesei(no)
handsome	hansamu(na)
hand-to-mouth	sono hi gurashi(no)
handwriting	hisseki; tegaki
handy	benri(na)
hang	(v.) tsurusu; kakeru; kakaru
hangover	hutsuka-yoi
haphazard	(n.) gūzen
	(adj.) gūzen(no)
	(adv.) gūzen ni
happen	okoru; gūzen ...suru
happy	kōhuku(na); ureshii; tanoshii
happy-go-lucky	rakutenteki(na)
harbor	(n.) minato
hard	(adj.) katai; muzukashii; tsurai
hardly	hotondo...nai
hardship	kon'nan
hardware	kanamono
harmful	yūgai(na)
harmless	mugai(na)
harmonious	chōwa shita; mutsumajii
harvest	(n.) shūkaku
haste	(n.) isogi
hat	bōshi
hate	hidoku kirau
haughty	gōman(na)
have	motteiru; motsu

have to do with	...ni kankei ga aru
hay fever	kahunshō
hazard	(n.) bōken; gūzen
he	(pron.) kare wa; kare ga
head	atama; zunō
headache	zutsū
headline	midashi
head office	honten; honsha
heal	iyasu; ieru
healthy	kenkō(na)
hear	kikoeru; kiku
heart	shinzō; kokoro; chūshin
heart attack	shinzō-mahi
heartbroken	kanashimi ni kureta
heartily	kokoro kara; zonbun ni
heat	(n.) netsu; atsusa
heating	danbō-sōchi
heaven	ten; tengoku
heavy	(adj.) omoi
heel	(n.) kakato
height	takasa
help	(v.) tetsudau; tasukeru
helpful	yaku ni tatsu
her	kanojo o; kanojo ni; kanojo no
herb	yakusō; kōsō
here	(adj.) koko ni; koko de; koko e
hereabout	kono atari de
hereafter	kongo
here and there	achikochi ni
heredity	iden; seshū
Here you are	Hai, dōzo; Sā, tsukimashita.
heritage	sōzoku-zaisan
hero	eiyū; shujinkō
hers	kanojo no mono
hesitate	tamerau
hiccup	(n.) shakkuri

	(v.) shakkuri o suru
hide	kakusu; kakureru
high	(adj.) takai
	(adv.) takaku
high-grade	kōkyū(na); jōshitsu(no)
high school	kōtō-gakkō
hill	(n.) oka; sakamichi
him	kare o; kare ni
hint	(n.) shisa
hip	denbu; oshiri
hire	(v.) yatou
his	kare no; kare no mono
historical	rekishiteki(na); rekishijō(no)
history	rekishi
hit	(v.) butsukaru; butsukeru
hobby	shumi
hog	buta
hold	(v.) motteiru; nigiru; daku
hole	(n.) ana
holiday	kyūjitsu; saijitsu
holy	shinsei(na)
home	(n.) ie; katei
homemaker	shuhu
hometown	hurusato
homework	shukudai
homogeneous	dōshitsu(no); dōshu(no)
homonym	doon-igigo
honest	shōjiki(na)
honey	(n.) mitsu
honeymoon	(n.) shinkon-ryokō; mitsugetsu
honor	(n.) meiyo
honorific	(n.) keigo
hook	(n.) tomegane; yōhuku-kake
hope	(n.) kibō
	(v.) nozomu; negau
hopefully	negawakuba

horizontal	(adj.) suihei(no)
horn	(n.) tsuno
horrible	hidoi; osoroshii
horse	(n.) uma
horseradish	seiyō-wasabi
hospital	byōin
hospitality	kantai; shinsetsu
hot	(adj.) atsui; karai
hot spring	onsen
hour	ichi-jikan; jikoku
house	ie
household	(n.) ikka; shotai
housewife	shuhu
housework	kaji
how	(adv.) don'na hū ni; don'na hōhō de
How are you?	Gokigen ikaga desu ka?
How do you do?	Hajime-mashite.
however	(conj.) shikashi
hug	(v.) dakishimeru
	(n.) hōyō
human being	ningen
humane	(adj.) jihibukai; shinsetsu(na)
humid	shikke no aru
humiliating	kutsujokuteki(na)
humorous	okashii; kokkei(na)
hundred	(n.) hyaku
hungry	kūhuku(na)
hurry	(v.) isogaseru; isogu
hurt	(v.) kizutsukeru
	(n.) kega; kutsū
husband	(n.) otto
hygienic	eiseiteki(na)
hymn	(n.) sanbika
hypnotism	saiminjutsu
hypocrite	gizensha
hypothetical	katei(no)

hysterical	hisuterikku(na); byōteki ni kōhunshita

I.
ice	(n.) kōri
icebox	reizōko
icicle	tsurara
idea	kangae
ideal	(adj.) risō(no); risōteki(na)
	(n.) risō
identification card	mibun-shōmeisho
identify	mimoto o akiraka ni suru
idiom	kanyō-goku
idle	(adj.) taida(na)
if	(conj.) moshi...naraba; ...ka dōka
ignorant	muchi(na); mugaku(na)
ignore	mushi suru
ill	(adj.) byōki de; kibun ga warui
illegal	(adj.) huhō(no); ihō(no)
illiterate	(adj.) monmō(no)
illustration	jitsurei; sashie; setsumei
image	(n.) zō
imagination	sōzō
imagine	sōzō suru
imitate	mohō suru
immaculate	ketten no nai
immature	mijuku(na)
immediately	sugu
immensely	hijō ni; kōdai ni
immersion	bottō
immigrant	(n.) ijūsha
immigrate	ijū suru
immoral	hudōtoku(na)
impolite	busahō(na)
import	(n.) yunyū
	(v.) yunyū suru
important	taisetsu(na)
impossible	hukanō(na)

impress	(v.) kandō saseru; inshō o ataeru
improper	hutekitō(na)
improve	shinpo suru
in	(prep.) ...no naka ni; ...ni; ...de
inadequate	hutekitō(na); hujūbun(na)
incapable	...dekinai
incense	(n.) kō
incident	(n.) dekigoto; jiken
incidentally	gūzen ni
inclination	keikō; konomi
include	hukumu; hukumeru
incoherent	tsujitsuma ga awanai
income	shūnyū
incompatible	mujun suru
incomplete	hukanzen(na)
inconsiderate	omoiyari no nai
inconvenient	huben(na)
increase	(v.) zōka suru; zōdai suru
incredible	shinji-gatai
indeed	(adv.) hontō ni
independent	(adj.) dokuritsu shita
index	(n.) sakuin; shishin
index finger	hitosashi-yubi
indicate	shiteki suru; shimesu
indifferent	mukanshin(na); reitan(na)
indigenous	dochaku(no)
indirectly	kansetsuteki ni
indispensable	hukaketsu(na)
individual	(adj.) kojin(no); koko(no)
individually	koko ni
indoor	okunai(no)
indulge	amayakasu; ...ni hukeru
industrious	kinben(na)
industry	sangyō; kōgyō
inevitable	hitsuzen(no)
inexpensive	yasui

inexpressible	iiarawase nai
infant	(n.) yōji
infection	densen; kansen
inferior	(adj.) ototta
infinite	(adj.) mugen(no)
inflammable	(adj.) kanensei(no)
influence	(n.) eikyō
	(v.) eikyō o oyobosu
inform	(v.) shiraseru
informal	hikōshiki(no); ryakushiki(no)
information	jōhō
informative	yūeki(na); chishiki o ataeru
inhale	(v.) suikomu
inherit	(v.) uketsugu; sōzoku suru
inhibit	kinshi suru
initiate	(v.) hajimeru
injection	chūsha
injure	kizutsukeru
inn	yadoya
inner	naibu(no)
innocent	(adj.) mujaki(na); keppaku(na)
innovation	kakushin; sasshin
inquire	tazuneru; toiawaseru
inquiry	toiawase; shitsumon
inquisitive	sensaku-zuki(na)
insane	ki ga chigatta
insect	konchū; mushi
insecure	huantei(na); huan(na)
insensitive	donkan(na)
insert	(v.) sōnyū suru
inside	(n.) uchigawa
insinuate	honomekasu
insist	shuchō suru
inspect	kensa suru; shisatsu suru
inspire	gekirei suru
instantly	sokuza ni

instead	kawari ni
instruction	kyōju; meirei; shiji
instructor	kyōshi; shidōsha
instrument	(n.) dōgu; gakki
insult	bujoku suru
insurance	(n.) hoken
integration	tōgō; yūwa; jinshu-sabetsu-teppai
integrity	kanzen
intellectual	(adj.) chiteki(na)
intelligence	chisei
intelligent	chiteki(na); sōmei(na)
intend	...suru tsumori de aru
intensive	(adj.) shūchūteki(na)
interaction	sōgo-eikyō
interchangeable	kōkan dekiru
intercultural	ibunka-kan(no)
interest	(n.) kyōmi; kanshin
interesting	omoshiroi; kyōmi aru
interfere	kanshō suru; samatageru
interior	(n.) naibu; shitsunai
intermediate	(adj.) chūkan(no)
intermission	kyūkei-jikan
international	(adj.) kokusaiteki(na)
internist	naikai
interpreter	tsūyaku
interrupt	samatageru; chūdan suru
intersection	kōsaten
intervene	kanshō suru; chōtei suru
interview	(n.) kaidan; kaiken
intestine	(n.) chō
intimate	(adj.) shinmitsu(na)
into	...no naka ni; ...no naka e
intonation	yokuyō
introduce	shōkai suru
intuition	chokkan
invade	shinryaku suru

invalid	(adj.) mukō(na)	
invaluable	hijō ni kachi aru	
invention	hatsumei	
invest	tōshi suru	
investigation	chōsa	
invisible	me ni mienai	
invitation	shōtai	
invite	(v.) shōtai suru	
invoice	(n.) okurijō	
involve	makikomu; hukumu	
iron	(n.) tetsu	
	(v.) airon o kakeru	
ironical	hiniku(na)	
irregular	(adj.) hukisoku(na)	
irrelevant	hutekisetsu(na); mukankei(na)	
irresponsible	musekinin(na); sekinin no nai	
irritate	iraira saseru	
island	(n.) shima	
isle	shima; kojima	
isolation	koritsu	
issue	(n.) ronten; mondai; hakkō	
it	(pron.) sore ga; sore wa; sore o; sore ni	
item	(n.) shinamono; kōmoku	
itself	sore-jitai	
ivory	zōge	
ivory tower	zōge no tō	
ivy	tsuta	

J.	jacket	(n.) uwagi
	jail	keimusho
	jam	jamu
	jam-packed	gyūgyū-zume(no)
	January	ichigatsu
	Japan	Nihon; Nippon
	Japanese	(n.) Nihongo; Nihonjin
		(adj.) Nihon(no)

Jargon	senmongo; chinpun-kanpun
Jaw	(n.) ago
Jealous	urayamashii; netamashii
Jeopardize	kiken ni sarasu
Jet lag	jisaboke
Jewel	(n.) hōseki
Job	(n.) shigoto
Jobless	shitsugyō shita
Join	(v.) kuwawaru
Joke	(n.) jōdan
	(v.) jōdan o iu
Journey	ryokō
Joy	yorokobi
Joyful	ureshii; tanoshii
Judge	(n.) saibankan
	(v.) hanketsu o kudasu; handan suru
Juicy	shiruke no ooi
July	shichigatsu
Jump	(v.) tobu
June	rokugatsu
Junior	(adj.) toshishita(no); kōhai(no)
	(n.) kōhai; (daigaku aruiwa kōkō no) san' nensei
Junior college	tanki-daigaku
Junior high school	chūgakko
Jury	baishin'in
Just	(adv.) chōdo; tan ni
Justice	seigi; kōhei; hanji
Justify	seitōka suru
Juvenile	(adj.) wakai

K.	keen	surudoi; hageshii
	keep	tamotsu; motteiru
	keep up with	tsuite-iku
	key	kagi
	key money	(shakuyanin ga shiharau) hoshōkin
	keystone	kaname-ishi

kick	(v.) keru
kid	(n.) kodomo
	(v.) karakau
kidnap	yūkai suru
kidney	jinzō
kill	korosu; kesu
kin	(n.) shinzoku
kind	(n.) shurui
	(adj.) shinsetsu(na); yasashii
kindergarten	yōchien
king	ō; kunshu
kingdom	ōkoku
kitchen	daidokoro
kite	(n.) tako
kitty	koneko
knee	hiza
knife	kogatana; hōchō
knock	(v.) tataku; utsu
know	(v.) shitteiru; shiru
knowledge	chishiki
L. label	(n.) harihuda; raberu
labor	(n.) rōdō; shigoto
	(v.) hataraku
laboratory	jikkenshitsu; enshūshitsu
lack	(n.) husoku
	(v.) husokushite iru
lacquer ware	shikki
ladle	(n.) hishaku; otama-jakushi
lady	hujin
ladies' room	hujinyō-tearai
lake	mizuumi
lamb	(n.) kohitsuji
land	(n.) tochi; kokudo
	(v.) jōriku suru; chakuriku suru
landlord	yanushi; jinushi

landmark	hyōshiki
landscape	(n.) keshiki
lane	(dōro no) shasen
language	gengo; kotoba
lap	(n.) hiza
large	(adj.) ookii; hiroi
last	(v.) tsuzuku
	(adj.) saigo(no); konomae(no); saikin(no)
	(adv.) saigo ni; saikin
lastly	saigo ni
late	(adj.) osoi; saikin(no)
	(adv.) osoku; osoku made
lately	chikagoro
later	(adv.) ato de
latitude	ido
latter	(adj.) kōsha(no); kōhan(no)
laugh	(v.) warau
	(n.) warai
laundromat	koin-randorī
laundry	sentakumono; sentakuya
lavatory	senmenjo
law	hōritsu
lawn	shibahu
lawyer	bengoshi
lay	(v.) oku; yokotaeru
layoff	ichiji-kaiko
lazy	taida(na)
lead	(v.) an´nai suru; tsūjiru
leader	shidōsha
leaf	(n.) ki-no-ha
leak	(v.) moreru; morasu
lean	motareru; katamuku
leap year	urūdoshi
learn	manabu; kikishiru
lease	(v.) chintai suru; chinshaku suru
least	(adj.) saishō(no)

leather	(n.) kawa
leave	(v.) saru; nokosu
	(n.) kyūka; kyoka
leave behind	okiwasureru; ato ni nokosu
lecture	(n.) kōgi; kōen
left	(n.) hidari
left-handed	hidari-kiki(no)
leftover	nokori-mono; tabe-nokoshi
leg	(n.) ashi
legally	horitsujō
legend	densetsu
legislator	kokkai-giin
legitimate	(adj.) gōhō(no); seitō(na)
leisure	(n.) hima; yoka
leisurely	(adv.) yuttari; nonbiri
lemon	remon
lend	kasu
length	nagasa
leopard	hyō
less	(adj.) yori sukunai
let	(v.) ...saseru; ...ni shiteoku
letter	(n.) moji; tegami
lettuce	retasu
leukemia	hakketsubyō
level	(n.) suijun; dankai
	(adj.) taira(na)
liable	sekinin no aru; manukarenai; ...shigachi(na)
liaison office	renraku-jimusho
liberal	(adj.) jiyū(na)
liberal arts	kyōyō-kamoku
liberty	jiyū
librarian	toshokan´in; shisho
library	toshokan; shosai
license	(n.) menkyo; kyoka
lick	(v.) nameru
lie	(n.) uso

	(v.) uso o iu
lie down	yokotawaru
life	inochi; seikatsu; jinsei
life belt	anzen-beruto; kyūmeitai
life insurance	seimei-hoken
life style	seikatsu-yōshiki
lift	(v.) mochiageru
light	(n.) hikari; akari
	(adj.) akarui; karui
lighthouse	tōdai
like	(prep.) ...no yōni; ...to dōyō ni
	(v.) konomu; ...suru no ga sukida
likes and dislikes	suki-kirai
lily	yuri
limit	(n.) genkai; seigen
line	(n.) sen; gyō; retsu
line up	ichiretsu ni narabu
linguistics	gengogaku
lining	uchigawa; uraji
linkage	tsunagari
lion	raion; shishi
lip	(n.) kuchibiru
lipstick	kuchibeni
liquid	(n.) ekitai
liquor	sake
listen	kiku
literacy	shikiji-ritsu
literally	mojidōri; mattaku
literature	bungaku
litigation	soshō
litter	(n.) gomikuzu
little	(adj.) chiisai; sukunai
	(adv.) wazuka ni
little by little	sukoshi-zutsu
little finger	koyubi
live	(v.) ikiru; seikatsu suru; sumu; sundeiru

	(adj.) ikiteiru; jikkyō(no)
livelihood	kurashi; seikei
lively	genki(na); kaikatsu(na)
liver	kanzō
living room	ima
living standard	seikatsu-suijun
load	(n.) tsumini; omoni
loan	(v.) kasu
local	(adj.) chihō(no); kakueki-teisha(no)
local train	futsū-densha; kakueki-teisha
location	basho
lock	(n.) jō
lodge	(v.) tomaru; tomaraseru
logical	ronriteki(na)
lonely	sabishii
lonesome	(adj.) sabishii
long	(v.) setsubō suru
	(adj.) nagai
	(adv.) nagaku
long-distance call	chōkyori-denwa
longevity	chōju
longitude	keido
long johns	momohiki
long-term	chōki(no)
look	(v.) miru; ki o tsukeru
	(n.) yosu; kaotsuki
look after	sewa o suru
look down upon	misageru; sagesumu
look for	sagasu
look forward to	tanoshimi ni shite matsu
look like	...no yō ni mieru
look up to	sonkei suru
lose	ushinau; makeru
loss	sōshitsu; songai
Lost and Found	ishitsubutsu-toriatsukaijo
lot	kuji; (tochi no) ikkukaku

lotus	hasu
loud	(adj.) sōzōshii; ooki
	(adv.) ōgoe de
love	(v.) aisuru; koi suru; konomu
	(n.) ai; aijō
lovely	(adj.) airashii; suteki(na)
low	(adj.) hikui
	(adv.) hikuku; kogoe de
lucky	un no ii
luggage	ryokō-kaban; tenimotsu
lukewarm	nurui
lullaby	komori-uta
lumber	(n.) zaimoku
luminous	sōmei(na); akarui
lump	(n.) katamari
lunar eclipse	gesshoku
lunch	(n.) chūshoku
lung	hai
luxurious	zeitaku(na)
M. machine	(n.) kikai
mad	(adj.) kichigai-jimita; muchū(no)
magazine	zasshi
magic	(n.) mahō; kijutsu
magnificent	subarashii; dōdōtaru
magnify	kakudai suru
maiden name	kyūsei
mail	(n.) yūbinbutsu
	(v.) yūsō suru
mailbox	yūbin´uke; posuto
mainly	shu to shite
maintain	iji suru
major	(adj.) shuyō(na)
	(n.) senkō-kamoku
	(v.) senkō suru
majority	daitasū

make	(v.) tsukuru; motarasu; suru
make up for	umeawase o suru
male	(n.) dansei; osu
malignant	yūgai(na); akusei(no)
mall	yanetsuki-shōtengai; shoppingu-sentā
mammal	honyū-dōbutsu
man	(n.) hito; otoko
management	kanri; keiei
mandatory	(adj.) kyōsei(no)
manipulate	atsukau; sōsa suru
mankind	jinrui
manly	otokorashii
man-made	jinkō(no)
manner	taido; gyōgi; hūshū
manpower	jinteki-shigen; rōdōryoku
manual	(adj.) te de suru
	(n.) tebiki
manufacture	(n.) seizō
	(v.) seizō suru
manuscript	genkō
many	(adj.) tasū(no)
map	(n.) chizu
maple	kaede; momiji
March	sangatsu
marginal	henkyō(no); heri(no)
mark	(n.) shirushi; konseki; (seiseki no) tensū
market	(n.) ichiba; shokuryōhin-ten
marriage	kekkon
married	kikon(no)
marry	kekkon suru
marvellous	subarashii; odorokubeki
mask	(n.) hukumen; kamen
mass	(n.) tasū; taryō; katamari
massive	tairyō(no); ganjō(na)
mass production	tairyō-seisan
master	(v.) shūtoku suru

masterpiece	kessaku
master's degree	shūshigo
match	(v.) tsuriau; niau
material	(n.) zairyō; shiryō
materialistic	yuibutsuronteki(na)
materialize	gutaika suru; jitsugen suru
mathematics	sūgaku
matter	(n.) jiken; mondai; busshitsu
matter-of-course	tōzen(no)
mattter-of-fact	jissaiteki(na)
mature	(adj.) enjukushita
may	...kamo shirenai; ...shite yoi; ...dekiru
May	gogatsu
mayor	shichō; chōchō
me	watashi o; watashi ni
meal	shokuji
mean	(v.) imi suru; ...suru tsumori de aru
meaningful	yūigi(na)
means	shudan; hōhō
measure	(v.) hakaru
meat	niku
mechanic	kikai-shūrikō
meddle	(v.) kanshō suru
medicine	igaku; kusuri
medieval	chūsei(no)
meditation	mokusō
medium	(adj.) chūkurai(no)
meet	(v.) au
meeting	kaigō; shūkai
mellow	(adj.) yoku jukushita; enjuku shita
melt	(v.) tokeru; tokasu
melting pot	rutsubo
memorial	(adj.) kinen(no)
memory	(n.) kioku
mend	(v.) naosu; tsukurou
men's room	danseiyō-tearai

mentally	seishinteki ni; chiteki ni
mention	(v.) iu; hanashi ni dasu
mentor	shidōsha; jogensha
merchant	shōnin
merciful	jihibukai
mere	tan'naru; hon no
merely	tan ni; tada
merit	(n.) chōsho; kachi
meritocracy	jitsuryoku-shakai
merry	yukai(na) ; yōki(na)
mess	(n.) konran; gotagota
message	dengon; shushi
metal	kinzoku
meteorologist	kishō-gakusha; tenki-yohōkan
method	hōhō; junjo
meticulous	sasaina koto ni ki o kubari-sugi no
microscope	kenbikyō
middle	(n.) chūō; chūkan
middle finger	nakayubi
midnight	mayonaka
might as well	...suru hō ga mashida; ...shita hō ga yoi
mighty	kyōryoku(na) ; hijō(na)
mild	odayaka(na)
military	(adj.) guntai(no); rikugun(no)
	(n.) guntai
milk	(n.) gyūnyū; miruku
Milky Way	ama-no-gawa
million	(n.) hyakuman
mimic	(v.) maneru
mincemeat	hikiniku
mind	(n.) seishin; kokoro; chiryoku
	(v.) kokoro ni kakeru; ki o tsukeru
mine	watashi no mono; tankō
mingle	mazeru; mazaru
minimum	(adj.) saisho(no)
minister	(n.) daijin; bokushi

minority	shōsūha; shōsū-minzoku
miracle	kiseki
mirror	(n.) kagami
miscellaneous	shuju-zatta(no)
mischievous	itazurazuki(na)
miserable	hisan(na); somatsu(na)
misfortune	hukō
misinterpret	gokai suru
misjudge	handan o ayamaru
miss	(v.) hazusu; hazureru; nogasu; ...ga inakute sabishii; natsukashigaru
missing	miataranai; kaketeiru
mission	shisetsu; dendō
mist	kiri; kasumi
mistake	(v.) machigaeru
	(n.) ayamari
misunderstand	gokai suru
mix	(v.) mazeru
model	(adj.) mohanteki(na); tenkeiteki(na)
moderate	(adj.) hikaeme(na); chūkurai(no)
modern	(adj.) gendai(no)
modest	(adj.) tsutsushimi-bukai; hikaeme(na)
moist	(adj.) shimetta
moment	shunkan
Monday	getsuyōbi
money	kinsen; okane
money order	yūbin-kawase
monkey	saru
monotonous	tanchō(na); taikutsu(na)
monster	kaibutsu
monthly	(adv.) maitsuki
moon	(n.) tsuki
morality	dōtoku
more	(adj.) sara ni ooi
	(adv.) motto; issō
more and more	masumasu

more or less	ōkare sukunakare
moreover	sono ue
morning	asa; gozen
morning sickness	tsuwari
mortgage	(n.) teitō
	(v.) teitō ni ireru
mosquito	ka
moss	koke
most	(adj.) taitei(no)
	(adv.) motttomo; hotondo
mother	haha; okāsan
mother-in-law	gibo
mother tongue	bokokugo
motive	(n.) dōki
motorcycle	ōtobai
mountain	yama
mouse	(n.) nezumi
mouth	(n.) kuchi
move	(v.) ugoku; ugokasu
movie	(n.) eiga
mow	(v.) kusa o karu
Mr.	...san
Mrs.	...san
Ms.	...san
much	(adj.) takusan(no)
muggy	mushiatsui
multinational	(adj.) takokuseki(no)
multiple	(adj.) tasū(no); hukugō(no)
murder	(n.) satsujin
	(v.) satsugai suru
murmur	(v.) tsubuyaku
	(n.) tsubuyaki; sasayaki
muscle	(n.) kin'niku
museum	hakubutsukan; bijutsukan
mushroom	kinoko
music	ongaku

must	(aux. v.) ...neba naranai; ...ni chigainai
	(n.) hitsuyōna mono
mustard	karashi
mutual	sōgōteki (na)
myself	watashi-jishin
mysterious	nazo (no); hukakai (na)
mythology	shinwa

N.

nail	(n.) tsume; kugi
naive	junshin (na); damasare-yasui
naked	hadaka (no)
name	(n.) namae
	(v.) nazukeru; shimei suru
namely	sunawachi
nap	(n.) hirune
narrow	(adj.) semai
nasty	hukai (na); iji no warui
nation	kokumin; kokka; minzoku
national	(adj.) kokkateki (na); zenkokuteki (na); kokuritsu (no)
national anthem	kokka
national flag	kokki
national holiday	kokutei-kyūjitsu
nationality	kokuseki
national park	kokuritsu-kōen
nationwide	zenkokuteki (na)
native	(adj.) seirai (no); dochaku (no)
natural	(adj.) shizen (no); tōzen (no)
natural resources	ten'nen-shigen
nature	shizen; seishitsu
naught	rei; zero
naughty	itazura (na)
near	(adj.) chikai
	(adv.) chikaku
	(prep.) chikaku ni; chikaku de
nearly	hotondo; ayauku
near-sighted	kinshi (no)

neat	kichin to shita; kogirei (na)
necessary	(adj.) hitsuyō (na)
necessity	hitsuyō; hitsujuhin
neck	(n.) kubi
need	(v.) hitsuyō to suru
needle	(n.) hari
negative	(adj.) hitei (no); hantai (no)
neglect	(v.) mushi suru
negligent	taiman (na); huchūi (na)
negotiate	kōsho suru
neighbor	(n.) rinjin
neighborhood	kinjo; hukin
neither...nor...	...demonaku, mata...demonai
nephew	oi
nervous	shinkeishitsu (na)
nest	(n.) su
neutral	(adj.) chūritsu (no)
never	keshite...nai; katsute...nai
nevertheless	sorenimo kakawarazu
new	(adj.) atarashii
newborn	umareta-bakari (no)
news conference	kisha-kaiken
New Year's Day	ganjitsu
next	(adj.) tsugi (no)
	(prep.) ...no tsugi ni
	(adv.) tsugi ni
nice	yoi; shinsetsu (na); kawaii
niece	mei
night	yoru
night school	yakan-gakkō
nine	(n.) kyū; ku
nineteen	(n.) jū-kyū; jū-ku
ninety	(n.) kyūjū
no	(adv.) (hiteibun no toi ni taishite) iie; (koteibun no toi ni taishite) hai
	(n.) hinin; kyohi; kinshi; hantai

noble	(adj.) mibun no takai; kōketsu(na)
nobody	(pron.) daremo...nai
nod	(n.) eshaku; unazuki
	(v.) unazuku
noisy	sōzōshii
nominate	(v.) suisen suru; ninmei suru
nonprofit	hi-eiriteki(na)
noodles	udon; soba
noon	shōgo; mahiru
normally	hutsū
north	(n.) kita
North Pole	hokkyoku
nose	(n.) hana
notable	kencho(na); chomei(na)
nothing	(adv.) sukoshimo...nai
	(n.) mu; zero
notice	(n.) chūi; tsūchi; keiji
	(v.) ki ga tsuku
notify	tsūchi suru
novel	(n.) shōsetsu
now	(adv.) ima; genzai
now and then	tokidoki
nowadays	chikagoro wa
nowhere	dokonimo...nai
nuclear	kaku(no); genshiryoku(no)
nuisance	meiwaku
numb	(adj.) shibireta; kankaku o ushinatta
numerous	tasū(no)
nurse	(n.) kangohu; hobo
nursery school	hoikuen
nursing home	rōjin-hōmu
nutritious	eiyō ni naru; jiyōbun no ooi
O. obey	hukujū suru
object	(n.) buttai; taishō; mokuteki
	(v.) hantai suru

objective	(adj.) kyakkanteki(na)
obligation	sekimu; gimu
oblige	yoginaku...saseru; arigatagaraseru
observe	kansatsu suru
obtain	te ni ireru
obvious	meihaku(na)
occasionally	tokidoki
occupation	shokugyō; senryō
occur	okoru; shōjiru
ocean	umi; taiyō
o´clock	ji
octopus	tako
odd	kisū(no); kimyō(na)
odor	nioi; kaori
offer	(v.) mōshideru; sashidasu
office	jimusho; kaisha; kanchō; kenkyūshitsu
official	kōshiki(no); kōmujō(no)
Off Limits	Tachiiri-kinshi.
often	shibashiba
oil	(n.) abura
oil painting	aburae
old	toshitotta; hurui
omit	nukasu; habuku
on	(prep.) ...no ue ni; ...no ue de
on and off	danzokuteki ni
on and on	yasumazu ni
once	(adv.) ichido; katsute
one	(n.) hitotsu; ichi
one after another	tsugitsugi to
one by one	junjun ni
onion	tamanegi
only	(adj.) yuiitsu(no)
	(adv.) tan ni; ...dake
open	(adj.) aiteiru; hiraiteiru
	(v.) akeru; hiraku
open-air	kogai(no)

operation	unten; sosa; shujutsu
opinion	iken
opinion poll	seron-chōsa
opportunity	kikai; kōki
opposite	(adj.) hantai(no); mukaigawa(no)
	(adv.) mukaigawa ni
	(prep.) ...ni mukaiatte
optimistic	rakkanteki(na)
or	aruiwa; sunawachi
orchard	kajuen
order	(n.) junjo; chitsujo; kaikyū; meirei
ordinary	(adj.) tsūjō(no); hutsū(no)
organize	(v.) soshiki suru; seiri suru
ornamental	sōshokuteki(na)
other	(adj.) betsu no
	(pron.) betsu no mono; betsu no hito
otherwise	samonai to
ought	...subeki de aru; ...no ga tōzen de aru
our	watashitachi no
ours	watashitachi no mono
ourselves	watashitachi-jishin
outdoor	kogai(no)
outgoing	(adj.) shakōteki(na)
outing	ensoku; sanpo
out-of-date	jidai-okure(no)
out of order	Koshōchū.
outside	(n.) gaibu; sotogawa
outskirts	kōgai; shūhen
outspoken	socchoku(na)
outstanding	kesshutsu shita; batsugun(no)
outwardly	gaimen wa
over and over	nandomo-nandomo
overcharge	(n.) hutō na nedan
over here	kochira ni; kochira de
over there	achira ni; achira de
overseas	(adj.) kaigai(no)

	(adv.) kaigai e
oversleep	nesugosu
overwork	(v.) hataraki sugiru
	(n.) karō
owe	kari ga aru
owl	hukurō
own	(adj.) jibun-jishin(no)
	(v.) shoyū suru
ox	oushi
oxygen	sanso
oyster	kaki

P.	Pacific Ocean	Taiheiyō
	pack	(v.) nizukuri suru; tsumeru; tsutsumu
	package	(n.) ni; tsutsumi
	pain	(n.) itami; kurushimi
	pain-killer	chintsūzai
	paint	(v.) egaku; nuru
	painter	gaka; penkiya
	palace	kyūden; daiteitaku
	pale	(adj.) aojiroi
	palm	(n.) te no hira
	pan	(n.) nabe
	panic	(v.) urotae saseru
		(n.) kyōhu; rōbai
	pants	zubon
	panty hose	pantē-sutokkingu
	paper	(n.) kami; shinbun; ronbun; shorui
	parade	(n.) gyōretsu
	paragraph	(n.) setsu; dan
	parallel	(adj.) heikō(no); ruiji(na)
	paralyze	mahi saseru
	paramount	saikō(no)
	paraphrase	(v.) betsu no kotoba de iikaeru
	parcel	(n.) kozutsumi
	pardon	(n.) yurushi

	(v.) kanben suru
parent	(n.) oya
parenthesis	kakko
park	(n.) kōen
	(v.) chūsha suru
parking lot	chūshajō
parliament	gikai; kokkai
part	(v.) wakeru; wakareru
participate	sanka suru
particular	(adj.) tokubetsu(no)
particularly	tokubetsu ni
pass	tōru; tōsu; gōkaku suru
pass away	nakunaru; shinu
pass by	tōri-sugiru
passageway	tsūro
passerby	tsūkōnin
passionately	netsuretsu ni
passive	(adj.) ukemi(no); shōkyokuteki(na)
past	(adj.) kako(no)
	(n.) kako
pastime	goraku; kibarashi
patent	(n.) tokkyo
path	michi
patient	(n.) kanja
	(adj.) gaman-zuyoi
patriotic	aikokushin no tsuyoi
pavement	hosō-dōro
paw	(n.) (inu, neko nado no) te-ashi
pay	(v.) harau
	(n.) kyūryō
payday	kyūryōbi
payment	shiharai
pea	endōmame
peace	heiwa
peaceful	heiwa(na); odayaka(na)
peach	momo

peacock	kujaku
pearl	(n.) shinju
peculiar	(adj.) dokutoku(no); hūgawari(na)
pedagogy	kyōjuhō; kyōikugaku
pedestrian	(n.) hokōsha
pedestrian crossing	ōdan-hodō
pediatrician	shōnikai
peel	(v.) kawa o muku
penalty	batsu
pencil	(n.) enpitsu
penetrate	tsuranuku; shimikomu; minuku
peninsula	hantō
pension	(n.) nenkin
people	(n.) hitobito; kokumin; jūnin
pepper	(n.) koshō
perceive	chikaku suru; kizuku
perfect	(adj.) kanzen(na)
perform	enjiru; jikkō suru
perfume	(n.) kōsui; kaori
perfunctory	ozanari(no); keishikiteki(na)
period	(n.) kikan; jidai; seiri
perm	(v.) pāma o kakeru
permanently	eikyū ni
permeate	shintō suru
permission	kyoka
permit	(v.) yurusu
perpetual	eikyū(no)
perplexed	tōwakushita; hukuzatsu(na)
persecute	hakugai suru
person	hito
personal	(adj.) kojinteki(na)
personality	jinkaku; kosei
personnel	jinji-bu
person-to-person call	shimei-tsūwa
perspective	tenbō
perspiration	ase

persuade	natokku saseru; settokushite...saseru
persuasive	settokuryoku no aru
pessimistic	hikanteki(na)
pesticide	sacchūzai
petroleum	sekiyu
pharmacy	yakkyoku
phenomenon	genshō
philosophical	tetsugakuteki(na)
philosophy	tetsugaku
phone	(n.) denwa
phoney	(adj.) itsuwari(no)
photo	(n.) shashin
photographer	shashinka
physical education	taiiku
physician	isha; naikai
physics	butsuri
physiology	seirigaku
pickle	(n.) tsukemono
pick up	hirou; te ni ireru
picture	e; shashin
pig	(n.) buta
pillow	makura
pine tree	matsu
pink	(n.) usu-momoiro
pioneer	(n.) kaitakusha; senkusha
pitch	(v.) nageru
pitiful	(adj.) ki no doku(na)
place	(n.) basho
	(v.) oku
placid	shizuka(na); ochitsuita
plain	(adj.) heii(na); kazari no nai; shisso(na)
plan	(n.) keikaku
	(v.) keikaku suru
plant	(n.) shokubutsu; kōjō
	(v.) ueru; maku; tateru
plaster	(n.) shikkui

plastic surgery	keisei-geka
plate	(n.) sara
play	(v.) asobu; ensō suru; enjiru
	(n.) asobi; shibai
pleasant	tanoshii; kimochi no ii
please	(v.) yorokobaseru
	(adv.) dōzo
plenty	(n.) takusan
	(adv.) jūbun ni
plump	(adj.) hukkura shita
plural	(adj.) hukusū(no)
pneumonia	haien
pocket money	kozukaisen
poem	shi; uta
poet	shijin
point	(n.) ten; kakushin; sentan
	(v.) sasu
poison	(n.) doku
pole	(n.) sao; bō
police	(n.) keisatsu
police officer	keisatsukan
police station	keisatsusho
policy	seisaku; hōsaku
polish	(v.) migaku
polite	reigi-tadashii; teinei(na)
political	seijijō(no)
political science	seijigaku
politics	seiji
pollution	osen; kōgai
ponder	jukkō suru
poor	mazushii; heta(na)
popular	ninki no aru; taishūteki(na)
population	jinkō
porcelain	jiki
pork	butaniku
port	minato

positive	kakujitsu(na); kōteiteki(na)
possess	shoyū suru
possibility	kanōsei
possible	(adj.) kanō(na)
postage	yūbin-ryōkin
postage stamp	yūbin-kitte
postal order	yūbin-kawase
postcard	hagaki
postgraduate	(adj.) daigakuin(no)
	(n.) daigakuin-sei
post office	yūbinkyoku
postpone	enki suru
potato	jagaimo; satsumaimo
potentiality	kanōsei
pottery	tōki
pour	(v.) sosogu
poverty	hinkon
powder room	keshōshitsu; hujinyō-tearai
powerful	chikara-zuyoi
practical	jitsuyōteki(na); genjitsuteki(na)
practice	(n.) renshū; kanshū; gyōmu
	(v.) renshū suru; jikkō suru
practice teaching	kyōiku-jisshū
praise	(n.) shōsan
	(v.) homeru
pray	(v.) inoru
precaution	yōjin; keikai
precede	senkō suru; sendō suru
precious	(adj.) kichō(na)
precipitation	kōuryō; kōsetsuryō
precisely	seikaku ni
preconception	sen'nyūkan
predict	yogen suru
preface	(n.) jobun
prefecture	to; hu; ken
prefer	...no hō o konomu

pregnant	ninshin shita
prehistorical	yūshi-izen(no)
prejudice	(n.) henken
preliminary	(adj.) yobi(no)
preparation	junbi; yōi
preparatory school	(shingaku-junbikō to shite no) watakushiritsu-kōtō-gakkō
prepare	junbi suru
prerequisite	(n.) hitsuyō-jōken
prescription	shohōsen
presence	shusseki; sonzai
present	(v.) okuru; teishutsu suru
preservation	hozon; hogo
preservative	(n.) bōhuzai
preserve	(v.) hozon suru; iji suru
preside	shikai suru
president	daitōryō; shachō; kaichō; (daigaku no) gakuchō
press	(v.) osu; appaku suru
press conference	kyōdō-kishakaiken
pressing	sashisematta
prestigious	meisei aru
presume	suitei suru; omou
pretend	huri o suru
pretty	(adj.) kawaii; kirei(na)
	(adv.) kanari; hijō ni
prevent	(v.) yobō suru; samatageru
previous	saki(no); izen(no)
price	nedan
priceless	nedan no tsukerarenai; taihen kichō(na)
pride	(n.) jisonshin; hokori
priest	seishokusha; shisai
primary	kisoteki(na); shuyō(na)
primary school	shōgakkō
prime minister	sōri-daijin
prime time	(terebi no) gōruden-awā
primitive	(adj.) genshiteki(na)

prince	ōji; kōtaishi
princess	ōjo; kōtaishi-hi
principal	(adj.) shuyō(na); dai-ichi(no)
	(n.) kōchō
principle	gensoku; shugi
printed matter	insatsubutsu
prior	(adj.) mae(no); saki(no)
priority	yūsenken
prison	keimusho
private	(adj.) shiteki(na); himitsu(no)
private enterprise	minkan-kigyō
private school	shiritsu-gakkō
privilege	(n.) tokken; tokuten
prize	(n.) shō; shōhin
probably	tabun
problem	mondai
procedure	tetsuzuki
process	(n.) katei; keika
proclaim	sengen suru; kōhyō suru
produce	(v.) tsukuru; seisan suru
product	seisanhin; seisakuhin
productive	seisanteki(na)
profession	shokugyō; kokuhaku
professional	(adj.) senmon(no); shokugyōteki(na)
	(n.) senmonka
professor	kyōju
proficient	(adj.) jukurenshita
profit	(n.) rieki
profitable	yueki(na)
profound	hukai; shin'en(na)
progress	(n.) shinpo
	(v.) shinpo suru
prohibition	kinshi
project	(n.) keikaku; jigyō
	(v.) keikaku suru
prolong	enchō suru; enki suru

prominent	takuetsu shita
promise	(n.) yakusoku
	(v.) yakusoku suru
promising	yūbo (na)
promote	sokushin suru; shōshin saseru
promptly	subayaku
pronunciation	hatsuon
proper	tekitō (na); tadashii
property	shisan; zaisan
prophetic	yogenteki (na)
proportion	hiritsu; wariai
proposal	teian; mōshide
prosperous	han'ei suru; yūfuku (na)
protect	hogo suru; mamoru
protein	tanpakushitsu
protest	(v.) hantai suru; kōgi suru
	(n.) kōgi
proud	hokori ni omou; jiman suru
prove	shōmei suru
proverb	kotowaza
provide	ataeru; sonaeru
provoke	shigeki suru; okoraseru
prudent	shinchō (na)
psychiatrist	seishinkai
psychological	shinriteki (na)
psychology	shinrigaku
psychotherapy	seishin-ryōhō
public	(adj.) kōkyō (no); kōzen (no); kōritsu (no)
public school	kōritsu-gakkō
public servant	kōmuin
publish	shuppan suru; kōhyō suru
pull	(v.) hipparu; hiku
pulse	(n.) myaku
pumpkin	kabocha
punctual	jikan-genshu (no)
punishment	batsu

pupil	seito; hitomi
purchase	(v.) kau
pure	junsui(na)
purple	(n.) murasaki
purpose	(n.) mokuteki
purposely	koi ni
purse	(n.) saihu; hando-baggu
pursue	ou; tsuikyū suru
push	(v.) osu
put off	enki suru
puzzle	(v.) komaraseru
Q. qualified	shikaku no aru; tekinin(no)
quality	(n.) shitsu
quantity	ryō
quarantine	ken'ekijo
quarrel	(n.) kōron
	(v.) kenka suru
quarter	(n.) yonbun-no-ichi
queen	(n.) jōō; ōhi
queer	(adj.) myō(na); hūgawari(na)
question	(n.) shitsumon; mondai
	(v.) shitsumon suru; utagau
questionnaire	shitsumonsho; ankēto
quick	(adj.) hayai
quickly	sugu ni
quiet	(adj.) shizuka(na)
quietly	shizuka ni
quit	(v.) yameru
quite	kanari; mattaku
quotation	inyō
quote	(v.) inyō suru
R. rabbit	usagi
race	(n.) jinshu
racism	jinshu-sabetsu

radiation	hōshasen
radical	(adj.) kyūshinteki(na); kageki(na)
railroad	(n.) tetsudō
rain	(n.) ame
	(v.) ame ga huru
rainbow	niji
rain check	shōtai no jun'en; uten-jun'en
rainy season	uki; baiuki
raise	(v.) mochiageru; okosu; tsunoru; sodateru
raisin	hoshi-budō
random	(adj.) teatari-shidai(no); detarame(na)
rank	(n.) kaikyū; mibun
ransom	(n.) minoshirokin
rapid	(adj.) hayai
rare	(adj.) mezurashii; namayake(no)
rat	(n.) nezumi
rate	(n.) wariai; ryōkin
rather	(adv.) mushiro; kanari
ratio	hiritsu; wariai
rationally	goriteki ni; riseiteki ni
raw	(adj.) nama(no)
razor	kamisori
reach	(v.) tōchaku suru; todoku
reaction	han'nō
read	(v.) yomu
ready	(adj.) junbi ga dekita
ready-made	kisei(no)
real	(adj.) hontō(no); genjitsu(no)
real estate	hudōsan
realistic	genjitsuteki(na); shajitsuteki(na)
realize	jitsugen suru; jikkan suru
really	jissai; hontō ni
rear	(n.) ushiro
reason	(n.) riyū
reasonable	dōri ni kanatta
reassure	anshin saseru

rebellious	hankōteki(na)
rebuild	saiken suru
recall	(v.) omoi-okosu
receipt	(n.) ryōshūsho
receive	uketoru; mukaeru
recently	saikin; chikagoro
reception desk	uketsuke
recess	(n.) kyūkei; kyūka
recession	keiki-kōtai
recognize	mitomeru
recollect	omoidasu
recommend	suisen suru
recommendation	suisenjō
reconcile	wakai saseru
reconfirm	saikakunin suru
reconsider	saikō suru
record	(v.) kiroku suru
	(n.) kiroku
recover	kaihuku suru
rectify	shūsei suru
red	(adj.) akai
	(n.) aka
red tape	kanryō-shiki; keishiki-shugi
reduce	(v.) heru; herasu
redundant	kudoi; jōman(na)
refer	genkyū suru; sanshō suru
reference	sanshō; sankō-bunken
reference book	sankōsho
refine	(v.) senren suru
reflect	han'ei suru; hansha suru
reflection	hansha
reformation	kaikaku; kakushin
refresh	arata ni suru; genki-zukeru
refrigerator	reizōko
refugee	bōmeisha; hinansha
refund	(v.) harai-modosu

refuse	kyozetsu suru
regain	torimodosu
regard	(v.) minasu; sonkei suru
regarding	...ni kanshite; ...no ten dewa
regardless of	...ni kakawarazu
region	chiiki; chiku
register	(v.) tōroku suru
registered mail	kakitome-yūbin
regret	kōkai suru; zan'nen ni omou
regularly	(adv.) kisoku-tadashiku; teikiteki ni
regulation	kisoku
reject	(v.) kyozetsu suru
rejoice	yorokobu
relationship	kankei
relative	(n.) shinrui
relatively	hikakuteki; sōtaiteki ni
relax	kutsurogu; yasumu
relevant	kanrenshita; tekisetsu(na)
reliable	shinrai dekiru
relieve	kaihō suru; anshin saseru
religion	shūkyō; shinkō
relinquish	hōki suru
reluctantly	shibu-shibu
rely	tayoru; ate ni suru
remain	(v.) nokoru; todomaru
remark	(v.) noberu
	(n.) iken; kenkai
remarkable	ichijirushii
remedy	(n.) chiryō; kyūsai-saku
remember	oboeteiru; oboeru
remembrance	kioku; kinen
remind	omoidasaseru
reminiscence	kaisō; omoide
remittance	sōkin
remote	tōi; henpi(na)
remove	(v.) torisaru; utsusu

renew	(v.) kōshin suru
nenovate	shūhuku suru; kakushin suru
rent	(n.) chintairyō
	(v.) chintai suru; chinshaku suru
repair	(v.) naosu
repeat	(v.) kurikaesu
replace	torikaeru
reply	(v.) kotaeru
	(n.) kotae
report	(v.) hōkoku suru; tsutaeru
	(n.) hōkoku; hōdō
report card	seisekihyō; tsūshinbo
represent	(v.) daihyō suru; arawasu
representative	(adj.) daihyōteki (na); dairi (no)
reproach	(v.) hinan suru
	(n.) hinan; chijoku
reproduction	saigen; saisei; seishoku
republic	kyōwakoku
reputation	hyōban
request	(v.) irai suru; mōshikomu
	(n.) irai; yōbō
require	yōkyū suru
required subject	hisshū-kamoku
requisition	(n.) yōkyū
rescue	(v.) sukuu
research	(v.) kenkyū suru; chōsa suru
	(n.) kenkyū; chōsa
resemble	niteiru
reservation	yoyaku; horyū; indean-hogokyojuchi
reserved	enryogachi (na); yoyakuzumi (no)
residence	jutaku
resign	jishoku suru; dan'nen suru
resist	(v.) teikō suru
resolution	ketsui
resolve	(v.) kaiketsu suru
resource	shigen; saichi

respect	(n.) sonkei
	(v.) sonkei suru
respectable	sonkei subeki
respectively	kakuji
respond	kotaeru; han´nō suru
responsibility	sekinin
responsible	sekinin no aru
rest	(n.) nokori; kyusoku
restaurant	resutoran; shokudō
restore	motodōri ni suru; kaihuku suru
restraint	yokusei; enryo
result	(n.) kekka
resume	tekiyō; rirekisho
retailer	kouri-shōnin
retire	intai suru; taishoku suru
retrospect	kaiko; tsuisō
return	(v.) kaeru; kaesu
reunion	saikai; shinbokukai
reveal	akiraka ni suru
revenue	shotoku; zeimusho
reverse	(v.) gyaku ni suru
review	(n.) kaiko; hukushū
revolutionary	(adj.) kakumeiteki(na)
reward	(n.) sharei; hōbi
rice	kome; gohan
rich	(adj.) kanemochi(no); megumareta
riddle	(n.) nazo
ride	(v.) noru; noseru
ridiculous	bakageta
right	(adj.) tadashii; migi(no)
right away	sugu
right here	chōdo koko de
right now	ima sugu
ring	(v.) naru; narasu
	(n.) yubiwa
ring finger	kusuri-yubi

riot	(n.) bodo; sodo
rip	(v.) yaburu; saku
ripe	(adj.) jukushita
rise	(v.) okiru; tachiagaru
risk	(n.) kiken
ritual	(n.) gishiki; shikiten
river	kawa
road	dōro
roast	(v.) yaku; aburu
robbery	gōtō
rock	iwa; ishi
roll	(v.) korogaru; korogasu
roof	(n.) yane
room	(n.) heya
root	(n.) ne; minamoto
rose	(n.) bara
rosy	barairo(no); yubō(na)
rot	(v.) kusaru; kusarasu
rotation	kōtai; junkan
rough	(adj.) arai
round	(adj.) marui
round-trip ticket	ōhuku-kippu
route	(n.) michi
routine	(n.) nichijō no katei; kimarikitta shigoto
row	retsu; narabi
royal	(adj.) ōzoku(no); ōritsu(no)
royalty	inzei; jōenryō
rub	(v.) kosuru
rude	soya(na); busahō(na)
ruin	(n.) hametsu; haikyo
rule	(n.) kisoku; shihai
	(v.) kitei suru; shihai suru
rumor	(n.) uwasa
run	(v.) hashiru
run out of	tsukai-hatasu
run short	husoku suru; kirashiteiru

rural	inaka(no)
rush	(v.) tosshin suru; tosshin saseru

S. Sabbath ansokubi

sabbatical leave	ichinen-yūkyū-kyūka
sacred	shinsei(na)
sacrifice	(n.) gisei; kenshin
	(v.) gisei ni suru
sad	kanashii
safe	(adj.) anzen(na)
	(n.) kinko
sailboat	hansen; yotto
saint	(n.) seijin; shito
sake	riyū; mokuteki
salad	sarada
salary	kyūryō
sale	hanbai; tokubai
salesperson	ten'in
salmon	sake; shake
salt	(n.) shio
salty	shio-karai
salutation	aisatsu
same	(adj.) doitsu(no); onaji
sample	(n.) mihon
sanction	(n.) seisai; bassoku
sanctuary	seiiki; chōjū-hogoku
sand	(n.) suna
sanitary	eiseijō(no); seiketsu(na)
sanitary napkin	seiriyō-napukin
sarcastic	hiniku(na)
satellite	(n.) jinkō-eisei
satisfactory	manzoku(na)
satisfy	manzoku saseru
Saturday	doyōbi
savage	yaban(na); mikai(no)
save	(v.) tasukeru; takuwaeru; habuku

savings account	yokin-kōza
saw	(n.) nokogiri
say	(v.) iu; noberu
saying	kotowaza
scald	(n.) yakedo
scallop	(n.) hotategai
scan	kuwashiku shiraberu; zatto miru; seimitsu-kensa o suru
scar	(n.) kizuato
scarcely	hotondo...nai; karōjite
scary	kowai
scatter	makichirasu
scenery	keshiki
scent	(n.) kaori; nioi
scheme	(n.) keikaku; keiryaku
scholar	gakusha; shōgakusei; tokutaisei
scholarship	shōgakukin
school	(n.) gakkō; ryūha
science	kagaku; shizen-kagaku
scientist	kagakusha
scissors	hasami
scold	shikaru
scrambled eggs	iritamago
scratch	(v.) kaku; hikkaku
scream	(v.) sakebu
	(n.) himei
screwdriver	neji-mawashi
scroll	(n.) makimono
sculpture	(n.) chōkoku; chōzo
sea	umi; taiyō
seafood	kaisanbutsu; gyokairui
sea gull	kamome
seal	(n.) natsuin; hūin
	(v.) han o osu; hū o suru
search	(v.) sagasu; shiraberu
seashore	kaigan
season	(n.) kisetsu; kōki

seat	(n.) zaseki
	(v.) chakuseki saseru
seaweed	kaisō
secluded	hitozato hanareta
second	(adj.) dai-ni(no); nibanme(no)
secondary school	chūtō-gakkō
second floor	nikai
secondhand	(adj.) chūko(no)
secret	(n.) himitsu
	(adj.) himitsu(no)
secretary	hisho
Secretary of State	kokumu-chōkan
security	anzen; hoshō
see	(v.) mieru; miru; wakaru; (hito ni) au
seed	(n.) tane
Seeing Eye dog	mōdōken
seek	sagasu; motomeru
seem	...rashii; ...to omowareru
See you	Sayōnara; Dewa mata.
segregate	bunri suru; jinshu-sabetsu o suru
seize	tsukamu; rikai suru
seldom	mareni; mettani...nai
select	(v.) erabu
selection	sentaku; senbatsu
self	(n.) jiko; jishin
self-centered	jiko-chūshin(no)
self-confident	jishin no aru
self-conscious	jiishiki no tsuyoi
self-controlled	jiseishin no aru
self-indulgent	wagamama(na)
selfish	rikoteki(na)
self-respecting	jisonshin no aru
self-righteous	dokuzenteki(na)
self-sacrificing	kenshinteki(na)
self-satisfied	jikomanzoku shita
sell	(v.) uru; ureru

sell out	urikireru
semester	(nigakki-seido no) gakki
senator	jōin-giin
send	okuru
senior citizen	rōjin
senior high school	kōtō-gakkō
sensible	hunbetsu no aru
sensitive	sensai (na)
sentence	(n.) bun; hanketsu
separate	(v.) wakeru; wakareru
sequence	renzoku; kekka
serene	odayaka (na); nodoka (na)
serious	majime (na); shinken (na); jūdai (na)
serve	(v.) kinmu suru; tsutomeru; kyūji suru
service charge	sābisuryō; tesūryō
sesame	goma
set	(v.) oku; sueru; sadameru; junbi suru
settle	(v.) ochitsuku; ochitsukaseru
settle down	ochitsuku; teiju suru
seven	(n.) nana; shichi
seventeen	(n.) jū-nana; jū-shichi
seventy	(n.) nanajū
several	(adj.) ikutsuka (no)
severe	kibishii
sew	nuu
sexism	sei-sabetsu
shade	(n.) hikage; hiyoke
shadow	(n.) kage
shake	yureru; yusuru
shallow	(adj.) asai
shame	(n.) haji; humenboku; hukō
shape	(n.) katachi
share	(v.) wakeru
sharp	(adj.) surudoi; kewashii; kibin (na)
shave	(v.) hige o soru
shaving	higesori

she	(pron.) kanojo wa; kanojo ga
sheep	hitsuji
shelf	tana
shell	(n.) kaigara
sheriff	hoankan
shift	(v.) kaeru; kawaru
shine	(v.) kagayaku
ship	(n.) hune
shipping	hunazumi
shirt	shatsu; wai-shatsu
shiver	(v.) hurueru
shoe	(n.) kutsu
shoot	(v.) utsu
shop	(n.) kouriten
shoplifting	manbiki
shopper	kaimono-kyaku
short	(adj.) mijikai; hikui; chikai; hūjibun(na)
	(adv.) mijikaku; hūjubun ni
shortage	husoku
shortcut	chikamichi
shortly	mamonaku; kantan ni
shortsighted	kingan(no)
shoulder	(n.) kata
shout	(v.) sakebu
show	(v.) miseru; an´nai suru; arawareru
show off	misebirakasu
shower	(n.) shawā; yūdachi
shrine	jinja
shrimp	koebi
shut	(v.) shimeru; shimau
shy	(adj.) uchiki(na)
sick	(adj.) byōki(no); unzarishite
side	(n.) waki; yoko
side by side	naran de
side effect	hukusayō
sight-seeing	kankō; kenbutsu

signature	shomei; sain
significant	jūyō(na); kencho(na)
signify	imisuru; shimesu
sign language	shuwa
silence	(n.) chinmoku; seijaku
silk	kinu
silly	(adj.) oroka(na)
silver	(n.) gin
	(adj.) gin(no)
similar	(adj.) ruiji(no)
simple	(adj.) tanjun(na); shisso(na)
simultaneous	dōji(no)
sin	(n.) tsumi
since	(conj.) ...shite irai zutto
	(prep.) ...irai
sincere	seijitsu(na)
Sincerely yours	keigu
sing	(v.) utau; saezuru
single	(adj.) tan´itsu(no); dokushin(no)
sink	(v.) shizumu; shizumeru
	(n.) (daidokoro no) nagashi
sister	shimai; shūdōjo
sit	(v.) koshi o kakeru
situation	jijō; jitai; basho
six	(n.) roku
sixteen	(n.) jū-roku
sixty	(n.) rokujū
size	(n.) ōkisa; sunpō
skill	ginō; tegiwa
skillful	jōzu(na); jukuren-shita
skin	(n.) hihu; kawa
skip	(v.) tobihaneru; shōryaku suru
sky	sora
sky blue	sorairo
skyscraper	kōsō-kenchiku
slang	(n.) zokugo

slantwise	(adv.) naname ni
sled	(n.) sori
sleep	(v.) nemuru
	(n.) nemuri
sleeping bag	nebukuro
sleeping car	shindaisha
sleepy	nemui; nemusō(na)
sleeve	sode
slender	hosoi; yaseta
slice	(n.) hitokire
	(v.) usuku kiru
slide	(v.) suberu; suberasu
slightly	sukoshi; wazuka ni
slim	(adj.) hossori shita
slip	(v.) suberu
slippery	suberu; tsurutsuru shita
slow	(adj.) osoi
	(adv.) yukkuri
slowly	yukkuri
small	(adj.) chiisai; sasayaka(na)
small change	kozeni
smart	(adj.) rikō(na)
smell	(v.) niou; kagu
smile	(v.) hohoemu
	(n.) hohoemi
smoke	(n.) kemuri; yuge
smoking	(n.) kitsuen
smooth	(adj.) nameraka(na)
smoothly	nameraka ni
snake	(n.) hebi
snapshot	(n.) sunappu-shashin
sneeze	(n.) kushami
	(v.) kushami o suru
snore	(n.) ibiki
	(v.) ibiki o kaku
snow	(n.) yuki

	(v.) yuki ga huru
snowman	yuki-daruma
snowstorm	hubuki
snuggle	yorisou; dakiyoseru
so	(adv.) sono yō ni; hijō ni
	(conj.) sono kekka
	(adj.) hontō de aru; sono tōri ni
soak	(v.) hitasu; nureru
soap	(n.) sekken
soap opera	renzoku-merodorama
sob	(v.) susuri-naku
sober	(adj.) majime(na); shirahu(no)
sociable	(adj.) shakōteki(na)
socialism	shakai-shugi
social welfare	shakai-hukushi
society	shakai
sociology	shakaigaku
soft	(adj.) yawarakai; onwa(na)
soft drink	seiryō-inryōsui
soil	tsuchi
sojourn	(n.) taizai
solar eclipse	nisshoku
soldier	(n.) heishi; gunjin
solemn	genshuku(na)
solid	(adj.) kengo(na); ganjō(na)
solitary	kodoku(na); sabishii
So long	Sayōnara.
solve	kaiketsu suru
some	(adj.) ikuraka(no)
	(adv.) tashō
somebody	(pron.) dareka
someday	itsuka
somehow	tomokaku; dōnika
something	(pron.) nanika; taishita-mono; taishita-hito
sometimes	tokidoki
somewhere	dokoka ni; dokoka e; dokoka de

son	musuko
song	uta
son-in-law	giri no musuko; musume-muko
soon	mamonaku; sumiyaka ni
sooner or later	osokare hayakare
soothe	nagusameru; yawarageru
sophisticated	senren-sareta
sophomore	(daigku, kōkō no) ni-nensei
sore	(adj.) itai; hirihiri suru
sorrow	(n.) kanashimi
sorry	kinodoku(na); mōshiwake nai
So so	Mā-mā desu.
soul	(n.) tamashii; kokoro
sound	(adj.) kenkō(na); kakujitsu(na)
sour	(adj.) suppai
source	minamoto
south	(n.) minami
souvenir	miyage
soy sauce	shōyu
space	kūkan; uchū
spacious	hirobiro to shita
Spanish	(n.) Supeingo; Supeinjin
	(adj.) Supein(no)
spare	(v.) kenyaku suru; (jikan o) saku
sparrow	suzume
speak	hanasu
speak out	hakkiri hanasu
speak to	hanashi-kakeru
special	(adj.) tokubetsu(no)
special delivery	sokutatsu-yūbin
specialty	senmon; tokusanhin; tokuseihin
specific	gutaiteki(na); tokutei(no)
spectacle	kōkei
spectacular	sōkan(na)
speech	kotoba; enzetsu
speed	(n.) sokudo

	(v.) isogu; isogaseru; supīdo o dasu
speed limit	seigen-sokudo
speedway	kōsoku-dōro
spell	(v.) (kotoba o) tsuzuru
spelling	go no tsuzuri
spend	(kane, jikan o) tsukau
sphere	tentai; chikyūgi; kyū
spicy	karai; kōbashii
spider	kumo
spill	(v.) kobosu; koboreru
spinach	hōrensō
spine	sebone; sekichū
spirit	(n.) seishin; kiryoku; rei
spiritual	(adj.) seishinteki(na); reiteki(na)
splended	kagayakashii; subarashii
split	(v.) saku; sakeru; wakeru
spoil	(v.) dame ni suru; amayakasu
spoken language	hanashi-kotoba; kōgo
spontaneous	jihatsuteki(na); shizen(na)
spot	(n.) chiten; shimi; oten
sprain	(v.) nenza suru
spread	(v.) hirogeru; hirogaru
spring	(n.) haru
spring roll	harumaki
sprinkle	(v.) furikakeru
square	(n.) seihōkei; hiroba
squeeze	(v.) nigiru; shiboru; warikomu
squirrel	risu
stable	(adj.) antei shita
staff	(n.) shokuin; buin
stain	(adj.) shimi; yogore
stair	kaidan
stamp	(n.) han; kitte; inshi
stand	(v.) tatsu; tatte iru
stand for	...o imi suru; ...o gaman suru; daihyō suru
stand up	tachiagaru

standard of living	seikatsu-suijun
stapler	hocchikisu
star	(n.) hoshi
stare	(v.) jirojiro miru; gyōshi suru
Star-Spangled Banner	seijōki; Beikoku no kokki
start	(v.) hajimeru; shuppatsu suru; bikutto suru
starved	ueta; himojii
state	(n.) jōtai; kokka; (Beikoko no) shū
	(v.) noberu
statement	seimei; chinjutsu
statesman	seijika
static electricity	seidenki
station	(n.) eki; teiryūjo; kyoku
stationery	bunbōgu
statistics	tōkei; tōkeigaku
statue	chōzō; sozō
status	chii; mibun
status quo	genjō
stay	(v.) taizai suru; todomaru
steady	(adj.) dōjinai; kenjitsu(na); antei shita
steal	(v.) nusumu
steam	(n.) jōki; yuge
steel	(n.) kōtetsu; hagane
steep	(adj.) kyū(na); kewashii
step by step	ippo-ippo
stepfather	gihu; keihu
stepping-stone	tobiishi; shudan
stereotyped	kata ni hamatta
stern	(adj.) genkaku(na)
sticky	nebaneba suru; mushiatsui
stiff	(adj.) kowabatta; (kata, kubi ga) kotta
still	(adj.) shizuka(na)
	(adv.) mada; soredemo
stimulate	shigeki suru
sting	(v.) (hari de) sasu
stipend	kyūryō; kyūhi

stir	(v.) kakimazeru
stockholder	kabunushi
stomach	(n.) i; hara
stomachache	hukutsū
stone	(n.) ishi; hōseki
stop	(v.) chūshi suru; chūshi saseru; tomaru; tomeru
storage	sōko; hokan
store	(n.) shōten
	(v.) takuwaeru
storekeeper	shōten-keieisha; tenshu
storm	(n.) arashi
story	monogatari; hanashi; uwasa
straight	(adj.) massugu(na); socchoku(na)
	(adv.) massugu ni; socchoku ni
strain	(n.) kinchō; karō
strange	mezurashii; hen(na); hushigi(na)
strategy	senryaku; sakuryaku
strawberry	ichigo
stream	(n.) ogawa; nagare
street	tōri; gairo
streetcar	romen-densha
stress	atsuryoku; kinchō; kyōchō
stretch	(v.) nobasu
strict	genkaku(na)
strike	(v.) utsu; ateru
striking	mezamashii
string	(n.) ito; hosohimo
string bean	saya-ingen; saya-endō
stripe	suji; shima
stroke	(n.) hossa; socchū
strong	(adj.) tsuyoi
structure	kōzō; soshiki
struggle	(v.) doryoku suru; kutō suru
	(n.) doryoku; huntō; teikō
stubborn	ganko(na)
student	gakusei; seito

student driver	jidōsha-unten reshūsei
student teacher	kyōiku-jisshūsei
studious	nesshin(na); benkyōka(no)
study	(v.) benkyō suru; kenkyū suru
	(n.) gakumon; kenkyū; shosai
stuff	(n.) zairyō
stuffy	kaze-tōshi no warui
stumble	(v.) tsumazuku; yorokeru; domoru
stylish	ryūkō(no); iki(na)
subconscious	(n.) senzai-ishiki
subcontract	(n.) shitauke-keiyaku
subject	(n.) shudai; gakka
subjective	shukanteki(na); kojinteki(na)
sublet	matagashi suru
submerge	hitasu; mienaku suru
submissive	jūjun(na)
submit	teishutsu suru; shitagau
subscribe	kōdoku suru
subsidize	hojokin o ataete josei suru
substance	busshitsu; honshitsu
substantially	jisshitsujō; jūbun ni
substitute	(v.) kaeru
	(n.) daiyōhin; dairinin
	(adj.) kawari(no)
subtitle	huku-daimoku; (eiga, terebi no) jimaku
subtle	bimyō(na); surudoi
subtract	hiku; genjiru
suburb	kōgai; kinkō
subway	chikatetsu
succeed	seikō suru; tsuzuku; keishō suru
success	seikō
such	(adj.) sono yō(na); kono yō(na); hijō(na)
such and such	...nado
such as	...no yōna
suddenly	toisuzen
suffer	kurushimu; nayamu

sufficient	jūbun(na)
sufficiently	jūbun ni
suffocate	iki ga kireru; chissoku suru; chissoku saseru
sugar	(n.) satō
suggest	shisa suru; teian suru
suicide	jisatsu
suitable	husawashii; tsugō ga yoi
sum	(n.) gōkei; yōten
summary	(n.) gaiyō; yōyaku
summer	(n.) natsu
summer time	natsu-jikan
summit	chōjō; shunō-kaidan
sun	(n.) taiyō
sunbathe	nikkō-yoku o suru
sunburn	(n.) hiyake
	(v.) hi ni yaku; hi ni yakeru
Sunday	nichiyōbi
Sunday best	yosoyuki no huku
sunflower	himawari
sunglasses	sangurasu
sunny	hi-atari no ii; akarui
sunny-side up	(adj.) medama-yaki(no)
sunrise	hi-no-de
sunset	hi-no-iri
super	(adj.) sugureta; gokujō(no)
superb	subarashii; mōshibun nai
superficial	hyōmen dake(no); senpaku(na)
superior	(adj.) sugureta
supervisor	kantokusha; shidō-shuji
supper	yūshoku
supplement	(n.) huroku; tsuika
supply	(v.) kyōkyū suru; hojū suru
support	(v.) shiji suru; huyō suru
suppose	katei suru; suisoku suru
supposedly	osoraku
supposing	...to katei sureba

suppress	yokuatsu suru; osaeru
supreme	(adj.) saikō(no)
supreme court	saikō-saibansho
sure	(adj.) tashika(na)
surely	tashika ni
surface	(n.) hyōmen
surgeon	gekai
surname	myōji
surplus	(n.) nokori; amari
surprise	(n.) odoroki
	(v.) odorokasu
surround	kakomu
survive	ikinokoru; nagaiki suru
suspect	(v.) ayashimu; utagau
suspended	enkishita; ryūhoshita
suspension bridge	tsuribashi
suspicious	ayashii
sustain	(v.) sasaeru; iji suru
swallow	(v.) nomikomu
	(n.) tsubame
swamp	(n.) numachi
swan	hakuchō
swear	(v.) chikau
sweat	(n.) ase
sweep	(v.) haku; sōji suru; issō suru
sweet	(adj.) amai; kawaii
sweetheart	koibito
sweet potato	satsumaimo
sweet tooth	amatō
swell	(v.) hukureru; hareru; zōdai suru
swiftly	hayaku; sugu ni
swim	(v.) oyogu
swimming	suiei; oyogi
swimsuit	mizugi
swing	(v.) yureru; yusuru
sword	katana

swordfish	mekajiki
syllable	(n.) onsetsu
syllabus	(kōgi no) gaiyō; kyōju-saimoku
symbol	(n.) shōchō; kigō
symbolize	shōchō suru; arawasu
sympathy	dōjō; awaremi
symptom	(byōki no) chōkō; shōjō
synonym	dōgigo
synthetic	gōsei(no); sōgōteki(na)
syrup	tōmitsu
systematically	soshikiteki ni; taikeiteki ni

T.	table	(n.) tēburu; shokutaku
	table d'hote	teishoku
	tactful	kiten no kiku; josai nai
	tactics	sakuryaku; senjutsu
	tag question	huka-gimon
	tag sale	(jitaku, toku ni garēji nado de okonau) chūkohin no yasu-uri
	tail	shippo; matsubi
	tailor-made	atsurae(no); chūmon-jitate(no)
	take	(v.) toru; eru; erabu
	take off	nugu
	take over	hikitsugu
	tale	hanashi; monogatari
	talented	yūnō(na)
	talk	(v.) hanasu
		(n.) hanashi
	talkative	hanashizuki(no); kuchikazu no ooi
	tall	(adj.) se no takai; takai
	tangerine	mikan
	tardy	(adj.) noroi; chikokushita
	tariff	kanzei
	tart	egui
	task	(n.) shigoto; ninmu
	taste	(n.) aji; konomi

	(v.) aji o miru
tasteful	shumi no yoi
tasty	oishii
tattoo	(n.) irezumi
tax	(n.) zeikin
tax-free	(adj.) menzei(no)
taxi	(n.) takushī
taxi-driver	takushī no untenshu
tea	ocha
tea ceremony	cha-no-yu
teach	oshieru
teacher	sensei; kyōshi
teacup	yunomi-jawan; kōcha-jawan
teahouse	kissaten
tear	(v.) saku; yaburu; yabureru
	(n.) namida
tease	(v.) karakau
technical	senmon(no); gijutsujō(no)
technology	kagaku-gijutsu
telegraph	(n.) denpō
telephone	(n.) denwa
	(v.) denwa o suru
telephone book	denwachō
television	terebi
tell	(v.) hanasu; iu; shiraseru
temperamental	okorippoi; kimagure(na)
temperature	ondo; taion
temple	tera; kyōkaidō
temporary	ichijiteki(na); kari(no)
ten	(n.) jū
tendency	keikō; seiheki
tender	(adj.) yasashii; yawarakai
tension	kinchō
tentative	kari(no)
term	(n.) kikan; kotoba; gakki
terminal	(adj.) owari(no); shūten(no)

term paper	gakkimatsu-repōto
terrible	(adj.) hidoi; osoroshii
territory	ryōdo; ryōiki
test	(n.) shiken; kensa
testimony	shōgen; hōkoku
textile	orimono
texture	kiji; tezawari
than	...yori mo
thank	kansha suru
Thank you	Arigatō gozaimashita.
thanks to	...no okage de
that	(adj.) ano; sono
	(pron.) are; sore
that is to say	sunawachi
That's right	Sono tōri desu.
theatre	gekijō; eigakan
their	karera no; kanojora no; sorera no
theirs	karera no mono; kanojora no mono
them	karera o; kanojora o; karera ni; kanojora ni;
	sorera o ; sorera ni
theme	rondai; wadai; shudai
then	sono toki; sore kara
theology	shingaku
theory	riron; gakusetsu; kenkai
therapy	chiryō
there	(adv.) soko e; soko de; soko ni
	(pron.) soko; asoko
therefore	sono kekka; shitagatte
thermometer	ondokei; taionkei
thesis	ronbun
they	karera ga; karera wa; kanojora ga; kanojora wa;
	sorera ga; sorera wa
they say	...to iu uwasa da; ...da sōda
thick	(adj.) atsui; koi; misshita
thief	dorobō
thigh	momo; daitaibu

thin	(adj.) usui; hosoi; mabara(na)
thing	mono; koto
think	(v.) kangaeru; omou
think highly of	sonkei suru
think little of	karonjiru
think of	...no koto o omou
think over	jukkō suru; yoku kangaeru
thinking	kangae; shikō
third	(n.) dai-san; sanban-me
thirsty	nodo ga kawaita
thirteen	(n.) jū-san
thirty	(n.) sanjū
this	(adj.) kono
	(pron.) kore; kono hito
this and that	areya-koreya
thoroughly	kanzen ni; jūbun ni
though	(conj.) ...da keredomo
	(adv.) demo; mottomo
thoughtful	omoiyari no aru; shiryo-bukai
thousand	(n.) sen
thousands of	ikusen no
thread	(n.) ito
threaten	odosu
three	(n.) san
thrill	(v.) zotto suru; zokuzoku suru
throat	nodo
through	(prep.) ...o tōtte; ...o hete
	(adv.) tōshite; zutto
throughout	(prep.) ...o tsūjite
throw	(v.) nageru
throw away	suteru
throw up	haku; ōto suru
thrust	(v.) tsukisasu
thumb	(n.) oyayibi
thunder	(n.) kaminari
Thursday	mokuyōbi

thus	kono yō ni
ticket	(n.) kippu
ticket office	kippu-uriba
tidal wave	tsunami
tidy	(adj.) kichin to shita; kogirei (na)
tie	(v.) musubu
tiger	tora
tight	(adj.) katai; kitsui; pittari shita
	(adv.) shikkari to; kitsuku; jūbun ni
till	...made
timber	zaimoku
time	(n.) jikan; kikan; jiki
time deposit	teiki-yokin
time difference	jisa
timely	(adj.) jiki o eta
	(adv.) oriyoku
timetable	jikokuhyō; jikanwari
timid	ki no chiisai
tiny	totemo chiisai
tip	(n.) chippu; kokoro-zuke
tired	tsukareta; akita
toast	(n.) kanpai
	(v.) kanpai o suru
tobacco	tabako
today	(n.) kyō
	(adv.) kyō; kyō wa
toe	(n.) ashi-yubi
together	(adv.) issho ni
tolerant	kandai (na)
tolerate	gaman suru
tollbooth	(yūryō-dōro no) ryōkinjo
tomato	tomato
tomb	haka
tomorrow	(n.) ashita
	(adv.) ashita wa
tongue	(n.) shita; kotoba

tonight	(n.) kon´ya
	(adv.) kon´ya wa
too	...mo mata; amari ni
tool	(n.) dōgu
tooth	(n.) ha
toothache	haita
toothbrush	haburashi
toothpaste	neri-hamigaki
top	(n.) chōjō; saikōi
	(adj.) saikō no
topic	rondai; wadai; yōshi
top secret	gokuhi(no)
tornado	tatsumaki
torture	(n.) gōmon; kunō
toss	(v.) nageageru
total	(n.) gōkei
totally	subete; mattaku
touch	(v.) sawaru; hureru
touchstone	shikinseki
tough	(adj.) katai; jōbu(na); kon´nan(na)
tour	(n.) kankō-ryokō; kengaku
tourist	kankō-kyaku
toward	...e mukatte; ...ni taishite
towel	(n.) taoru; tenugui
tower	(n.) tō; tawā
town	machi
town hall	machi-yakuba
trace	(n.) ashiato; keiseki
trade	(v.) baibai suru
	(n.) shōgyō; bōeki
tradition	kanshū; dentō
traditional	dentōteki(na)
traffic	(n.) kōtsū; unyu
traffic light	kōtsū-shingō
tragic	higekiteki(na)
train	(n.) densha; ressha

training	renshū; yōsei
trait	tokuchō
tranquil	shizuka(na)
transaction	shori; torihiki
transcript	seiseki-shōmeisho
transfer	(v.) utsusu; norikaeru
transfusion	yuketsu; chūnyū
transit passenger	noritsugi-kyaku
translate	yakusu
translation	honyaku
transparent	tōmei(na)
transplant	(v.) ishoku suru
transportation	yusō; yusō-kikan
trash	(n.) kuzu
travel	(n.) ryokō
	(v.) ryokō suru
travel agency	ryokō-dairiten
traveler	ryokōsha
traveler's check	ryokōshayō-kogitte
tray	bon
treasure	takara
treat	(v.) tori-atsukau; shori suru; gochisō suru
	(n.) motenashi; ogori
tree	(n.) ki; jumoku
tremble	(v.) hurueru
tremendous	subarashii; monosugoi
trend	(n.) jōsei; ryūkō
trespass	(v.) shin'nyū suru; shingai suru
	(n.) huhō-shin'nyū
trial	tameshi; shiren; saiban
trial and error	shikō-sakugo
triangle	sankakukei
tribe	shuzoku; buzoku
trick	(n.) sakuryaku; itazura; tejina
tricky	zurui; te no konda
trip	(n.) ryokō

triumphantly	ikiyōyō to; kachi-hokotte
trivial	tsumaranai; sasai(na)
tropical	nettaiteki(na)
trouble	(n.) shinpai; mendō; meiwaku
	(v.) meiwaku o kakeru; nayamasu
trousers	(n.) zubon
trout	masu
true	(adj.) shinjitsu(no); honmono(no)
truehearted	seijitsu(na)
trust	(v.) shinrai suru
trustworthy	kakujitsu(na); shinrai dekiru
truth	shinjitsu; jijitsu
try	(v.) yatte-miru
try on	shichaku suru
Tuesday	kayōbi
tulip	chūrippu
tune	(n.) chōshi; hushi
turkey	shichimenchō
turmoil	konran; sōdō
turn	(v.) mawaru; mawasu
turn off	(suidō, gasu nado o) tomeru; (TV, dentō nado o) kesu
turn on	(suidō, gasu nado o) dasu; (TV, dentō nado o) tsukeru
turn over	(peji o) mekuru; negaeri o utsu
turnpike	yuryō-dōro
turtle shell	bekkō
tutor	(n.) katei-kyōshi; kojin-shidō-kyōkan
twelve	(n.) jū-ni
twenty	(n.) nijū
twice	nido; nibai; nijū
twin	(n.) hutago
twinkle	(v.) kirameku
twist	(v.) nejiru; yugameru
two	(n.) ni
typhoon	taihū
typical	tenkeiteki(na); daihyōteki(na)
tyranny	sensei-seiji; assei

U.	ugly	minikui
	ultimately	kekkyoku
	umbrella	amagasa
	unable	dekinai
	unacceptable	uketorigatai; shōchi dekinai
	unaccustomed	hunare(no)
	unanimous	manjō-icchi(no); gōi(no)
	unavailable	erarenai; riyō dekinai; huzai(no)
	unaware	kizukanai
	unbalanced	hukinkō(na)
	unbearable	taegatai
	unbelievable	shinjigatai
	unbutton	botan o hazusu
	uncertain	hutashika(na)
	unchanged	kawaranai
	uncle	oji
	unclean	huketsu(na); yogoreta
	uncomfortable	kokochi-yokunai
	uncommon	(adj.) mezurashii; hibon(na)
	unconcerned	mukanshin(na); mukankei(na)
	unconditional	mujōken(no)
	unconnected	kanren no nai
	unconsciously	muishiki ni
	uncontrollable	yokusei dekinai
	uncooked	nama(no)
	uncountable	(adj.) kazoerarenai
	uncover	akiraka ni suru; ooi o toru
	under	(prep.) ...no shita ni; ...ika no; ...chū; ...no moto ni
	underestimate	yasuku mitsumoru; kashō-hyōka suru
	undergo	keiken suru
	undergraduate	(daigaku no) gakubu-gakusei
	underground	(adj.) chika(no)
	underline	(n.) kasen
		(v.) kasen o hiku
undershirt	hadagi

understand	rikai suru; shōchi-shiteiru
understandable	rikai dekiru
understanding	(n.) rikai; chiryoku; ryōkai
understudy	(n.) daiyaku-haiyū
underwear	shitagi; hadagi
undesirable	nozomashiku-nai
undeveloped	mikaihatsu(no); mihattatsu(no)
undo	torikesu; hodoku; nugu; horobosu
undress	(v.) nugu; hōtai o toru
undrinkable	nomenai
uneasy	huan(na); muzukashii
uneatable	taberarenai
uneducated	kyōiku no nai
unemployed	shitsugyō-shita
unemployment benefit	shitsugyō-teate
unequal	hitoshikunai; hukōhei(na)
uneven	taira de nai; ichiyō de nai
unexpectedly	omoigakenaku
unexpressed	hyōgen-sarenai
unfair	hukōhei(na)
unfaithful	huseijitsu(na)
unfamiliar	narete-inai; huan'nai(na)
unfold	hiraku
unforgettable	wasurerarenai
unfortunate	(adj.) huun(na)
unfriendly	hushinsetsu(na)
unhappy	hukō(na); kanashii
uniformly	ichiyō ni
unimportant	jūyō de nai
unique	murui(no); mezurashii
united	ketsugō-shita
universal	huhenteki(na); bankoku(no); uchū(no)
university	sōgō-daigaku
unjust	husei(na); hukōhei(na)
unkind	hushinsetsu(na)
unknown	(adj.) michi(no); mumei(no)

unlike	(adj.) nite-inai
	(prep.) ...to chigatte
unlikely	(adj.) arisō mo nai; kangaerarenai
unload	ni o orosu
unlock	kagi o akeru
unlucky	un no warui
unmarried	mikon(no)
unnatural	hushizen(na)
unnecessary	huhitsuyō(na)
unofficial	hikōshiki(no)
unpack	(tsutsumi, ni o) toku
unpleasant	huyukai(na)
unpredictable	yosoku dekinai
unprofitable	rieki no nai
unreasonable	hugōri(na)
until	(conj.) ...suru made
	(prep.) ...made zutto
unusual	hutsū de nai; kawatta
unwillingly	hushō-bushō
unworthy	ataishinai
upbringing	shitsuke; yōiku
update	(v.) saishin ni suru
uphill	(adj.) noborizaka(no)
uphold	sasaeru
upper class	jōryū-kaikyū
upright	(adj.) suichoku(na)
	(adv.) suichoku ni
ups and downs	kihuku; seisui
upset	(adj.) rōbai-shite; konran-shite
upside-down	(adj.) sakasama(no)
	(adv.) sakasama ni
upstairs	(n.) nikai; kaijō
	(adv.) nikai ni; nikai de
up there	mukō ni; mukō de
uptight	(adj.) kinchōshita; irairashita
up to	...made

up-to-date	saikin(no)
uptown	(n.) yamanote
urban	tokai(no); tokaihū(no)
urbanization	toshika
urge	(v.) sekitateru; unagasu
urgent	kinkyū(no)
urine	nyō
us	watashitachi o; watashitachi ni
usage	tsukai-kata
use	(n.) shiyō; riyō
	(v.) tsukau
used	(adj.) chuko(no)
useful	yaku ni tatsu
useless	yaku ni tatanai
usually	tsujō; hutsū
utmost	(adj.) saikō(no); saidai(no)
utopia	risōkyō
utter	(v.) iu

V.	vacant	kara(no); aiteiru
	vacation	(n.) kyūka
	vaccination	shutō
	vacuum cleaner	shinkū-sōjiki
	vague	aimai(na)
	vain	muda(na); kūkyo(na)
	valid	yūkō(na); seitō(na); gōhōteki(na)
	valley	tanima
	valuable	kōka(na); kichō(na)
	value	(n.) kachi

vanish	kieru
various	samazama(na)
vary	tayō ni suru; henka suru
vase	kabin
vast	(adj.) kōdai(na); kyodai(na)

vegetable	yasai; shokubutsu
vegetarian	saishoku-shugisha
vehicle	kuruma
vein	kekkan; jōmyaku
vending machine	jidō-hanbaiki
ventilation	kanki-sōchi
verbal	(adj.) kotoba(no)
verify	shōmei suru
verisimilitude	hakushinsei; shinjitsu-rashisa
vernal equinox	shunbun
verse	shi; inbun
version	honyaku; yakusho
vertical	(adj.) suichoku(no)
very	(adv.) hijō ni
veterinarian	jūi
veto	(n.) kyohiken
vice-president	huku-daitōryō; huku-shachō; huku-gakuchō
vice versa	gyaku mo mata dōyō
vicinity	hukin; kinrin
victim	higaisha; giseisha
victory	shori
view	(n.) tenbō; kenkai; shiya
viewpoint	kenkai
vigorous	chikara-zuyoi; genki(na)
village	mura
vinegar	su
vineyard	budōen
violate	(v.) (hō, keiyaku nado o) yaburu; (jiyū, himitsu nado o) shingai suru
violent	ranbō(na); hageshii
virtue	toku; biten
visa	(n.) biza; sashō
vis-a-vis	(adv.) mukai-atte
visible	me ni mieru; meihaku(na)
vision	(n.) shiryoku; dosatsuryoku; gen'ei
visit	(v.) hōmon suru; asobi ni iku

	(n.) hōmon; mimai; kenbutsu
visiting card	meishi
vitality	seimeiryoku; katsuryoku
vitamin	bitamin
vivid	azayaka(na); ikiikishita
vocabulary	goi
vocation	tenshoku; shokugyō
voice	(n.) koe
void	(adj.) kara(no); mukō(na)
volcano	kazan
voluntarily	jihatsuteki ni
volunteer	(v.) susunde...suru; shigan suru
	(n.) shigansha; yūshisha
vomit	(v.) ōto suru
vote	(n.) hyōketsu; senkyoken
	(v.) tōhyō suru
vow	(v.) chikau
	(n.) seiyaku; chikai
vowel	boin
voyage	(n.) kōkai; sora no tabi
vulgar	soya(na); gehin(na)
vulnerable	kōgeki-sareyasui

W.

wage	(n.) chingin; kyūryō
waist	koshi; yōbu
wait	(v.) matsu
waiting room	machiai-shitsu
wake up	me ga sameru; okiru; okosu
walk	(v.) aruku; aruiteiku
	(n.) sanpo
walking stick	tsue
wall	(n.) kabe; hei
wallet	saihu
wander	(v.) samayou; aruki-mawaru
want	(v.) nozomu; ...shitai; ...shite moraitai; hitsuyō de aru

war	(n.) sensō
ward	(n.) byōtō; kanbō
warehouse	sōko
warm	(adj.) atatakai; atsui; omoiyari no aru
	(v.) atatameru; atatamaru
warn	keikoku suru
warrant	(n.) hoshō; konkyo; kyoka
wash	(v.) arau; sentaku suru
washing machine	sentakuki
waste	(v.) rōhi suru; shōmō suru
wastepaper basket	kamikuzu-kago
watch	(v.) jitto miru; sewa suru; keikai suru
	(n.) kaichū-dokei; ude-dokei; keikai
water	(n.) mizu
	(v.) mizu o yaru
water closet	suisenshiki-tearai
watercolor	suisaiga
waterfall	taki
water lily	suisen
watermelon	suika
waterproof	(adj.) bōsui(no)
watery	mizuppoi; shimeppoi
wave	(n.) nami
wax	rō
way	(n.) michi; yarikata; hōmen; shūkan
we	watashitachi ga; watashitachi wa
weak	yowai
weak point	jakuten
wealthy	yūfuku(na)
weapon	buki
wear	(v.) kiru; mi ni tsukeru
wear out	kihurusu; shōmō suru
weary	(adj.) tsukareta; taikutsu(na)
weather	(n.) tenki; kishō
weather forecast	tenki-yohō
wedding	kekkon; kekkonshiki

Wednesday	suiyōbi
weed	(n.) zassō
week	shū; isshūkan
weekday	shūjitsu
weekend	(n.) shūmatsu
weekly	(adj.) shū ni ichido(no)
	(adv.) shū-ikkai
weep	naku
weight	(n.) omosa
welcome	(int.) yōkoso; irrashai
	(adj.) kangei sareru
	(v.) kangei suru
welfare	hukushi; kōsei
well	(adv.) yoku; jōzu ni; jūbun ni
	(adj.) kenkō(na); kibun ga yoi; manzoku subeki
well-balanced	tsuriai no toreta
well-done	jūbun ni yaketa; yoku dekita
well-dressed	minari no kichin to shita
well-informed	hakushiki(no); jōhō ni tsūjita
well-known	yoku shirareta
well-mannered	gyōgi no yoi; jōhin(na)
west	(n.) nishi; nishigawa
western	(adj.) nishi(no); seibu(no)
westernize	seiyōka suru
wet	(adj.) nureta; shimetta
whale	(n.) kujira
wharf	(n.) hatoba
what	(pron.) nani; nanimono; nanigoto; dono kurai
	(adj.) nan'no; nan to iu; don'na; dono
what about	...wa dō desu ka.
whatever	(pron.) ...wa nan demo; ika ni ...demo
	(adj.) tatoe...demo; don'na...demo
what for	dōshite
what is called	iwayuru
what is more	sono ue
wheat	komugi

wheelchair	kuruma-isu
when	(adv.) itsu
	(conj.) ...suru toki ni
whenever	(conj.) ...suru toki wa itsu demo
where	(adv.) doko ni; doko de; doko e
	(pron.) doko
	(conj.) ...suru tokoro ni; ...suru tokoro de
wherever	(adv.) ...suru tokoro wa doko demo
whether	(conj.) ...ka dōka
which	(pron.) dochira; dore; dono-hito; ...suru tokoro no; soshite sore wa; shikashi sore wa
	(adj.) dochira no; dono
whichever	(pron.) ...suru dore demo; dochira ga...suru to shitemo
	(adj.) dono...demo; ittai dochira no
while	(conj.) ...suru ma ni; soshite ippō
	(n.) jikan; kikan; ma
whisper	(v.) sasayaku
whistle	(v.) kuchibue o huku; hyū to naru
	(n.) kuchibue; keiteki
white	(adj.) shiroi
	(n.) shiro
white lie	akui no nai uso
who	(pron.) dareka; dare ga; soshite sono hito wa
whoever	...suru tokoro no hito wa dare demo; tatoe dare ga ...demo
whole	(adj.) zentai(no); kanzen(na)
	(n.) zentai; zenbu
wholeheartedly	kokoro o komete
wholesale	(n.) oroshiuri
who's who	shinshi-roku; meishi-roku
why	(adv.) dōshite; naze...ka to iu riyū
why don't you	...shite wa dō desu ka.
Why not	Ii desu-yo.
wide	(adj.) hiroi
widespread	(adj.) hiromatta

widow	mibōjin
width	hirosa; haba
wife	tsuma; kanai
wild	(adj.) yasei(no); shizen no mama(no); ranbō(na)
will	(n.) ishi; yuigonsho
willingly	yorokon de
win	(v.) katsu; kakutoku suru
wind	(n.) kaze
window	mado
windowpane	mado-garasu
windy	kaze no tsuyoi
wine	(n.) budōshu
wing	(n.) tsubasa; tōha
winter	(n.) huyu
wipe	(v.) nuguu; hukitoru; kesu
wire	(n.) harigane
wisdom	chie; hunbetsu
wise	(adj.) kenmei(na); hakugaku(na)
wish	(v.) negau; ...de areba ii to omou
	(n.) negai; inori
wit	(n.) kichi; tonchi
with	(prep.) ...to issho ni; ...o motte; ...o tsukatte
withdraw	(v.) hikkomeru; hikkomu; hikidasu
within	(prep.) ...no uchi ni; ...inai ni
without	(prep.) ...no soto ni; ...nashi de
witness	(n.) shōgen; mokugekisha
woman	Josei; hujin
womanly	on'na-rashii
women's liberation	Josei-kaihō-undō
wonder	(n.) kyōi; hushigi
	(v.) odoroku; kanshin suru; hushigi ni omou;
	...kashira to omou
wonderful	subarashii
wood	mokuzai; mori
wool	yōmō; keorimono
word	(n.) tango; kotoba

word order	gojun
wordy	kotoba no ooi; jōman(na)
work	(n.) shigoto; sakuhin
	(v.) shigoto o suru; benkyō suru; hatarakaseru
workshop	shigotoba; kenkyūkai; kōshūkai
world	sekai; yono-naka
worldly	sezokuteki(na)
world war	sekai-taisen
worldwide	sekaiteki(na)
worm	(n.) mushi; mimizu
worry	nayamasu; nayamu; shinpai suru
worse	(adj.) issō-warui
worship	(n.) sūhai
worst	(adj.) saiaku(no)
worthwhile	kachi no aru
worthy	(adj.) kachi no aru; ...ni husawashii
would rather	mushiro...suru
wound	(n.) kizu; hushō
wrap	(v.) tsutsumu
wrapping cloth	huroshiki
wrinkle	(n.) shima; hida
wrist	tekubi
wristwatch	ude-dokei
write	(v.) kaku
written examination	hikki-shiken
wrong	(adj.) machigatta; husei(na); gyaku(no); koshō no aru
wrong number	machigai-denwa
X. x-ray	(v.) x-sen shashin o toru; rentogen-satsuei o suru
Y. yard	(n.) niwa
yawn	(n.) akubi
	(v.) akubi o suru
year	toshi
year after year	nen-nen

yearbook	nenkan; nenpō
yearly	(adj.) nen-ikkai(no); reinen(no)
	(adv.) nen ni ichido
yearning	akogare
yellow	(adj.) kiiro(no)
	(n.) kiiro
yen	(Nihon no tsūka-tan´i) En
yesterday	(n.) kinō; sakujitsu
	(adj.) kinō(no)
	(adv.) kinō; sakujitsu
yet	mada; mō; soredemo nao
yield	(v.) sanshutsu suru; motarasu; ataeru
yolk	ran´ō; kimi
you	anata ga; anata wa; anata o; anata ni
young	(adj.) wakai; toshi-shita(no)
your	anata no
yours	anata no mono
Yours truly	keigu
yourself	anata-jishin
youth	wakasa; seinen
youthful	wakawakashii

Z. zenith	chōten; zecchō
zero	(n.) rei; zero
zip code	yubin-bangō
zoo	dobutsuen
zzz	(ibiki no oto) gūgū

Look and Say: Quick References

[Socializing]

Yes.	Hai.
No.	Iie.
Please.	Onegai-shimasu.
Nice to meet you.	Hajime-mashite.
I'm Kate Smith.	Kate Smith desu.
How are you?	Gokigen ikaga desu ka?
May I have your name, please?	O-namae o oshiete itadake-masu ka?
Good morning.	Ohayō-gozaimasu.
Good afternoon.	Kon'nichiwa.
Good evening.	Konbanwa.
Good night.	Oyasumi-nasai.
Good-bye.	Sayōnara.
Thank you.	Arigatō-gozaimasu.
You're welcome.	Dōitashi-mashite.
Excuse me. /Sorry.	Sumimasen.
Say it one more time, please.	Mō ichido onegai-shimasu.
Thank you for the meal. (Before eating.)	Itadaki-masu.
Thank you for the meal. (After eating.)	Gochisōsama-deshita.
Do you speak English?	Eigo o hanashi-masu ka?
I understand Japanese a little.	Nihongo wa, sukoshi wakari-masu.

[For Emergencies]

110(Police)	Hyaku-tō-ban(Keisatsu)
119(Fire Station & Ambulance)	Hyaku-jūkyū-ban(Shōbōsho & Kyūkyūsha)
Call the police, please.	Keisatsu onegai-shimasu.
Call an ambulance, please.	Kyūkyūsha o yonde-kudasai.

[At A Hospital]

Do you have any doctors who speak English?	Eigo no dekiru sensei irasshai-masu ka?
I have a pain in my chest.	Kyōbu ga itami-masu.

I feel sick.	Hakike ga shimasu.
I have a fever.	Netsu ga arimasu.
I have a headache.	Zutsū ga shimasu.
I have a stomachache.	Hukutsū ga shimasu.
I have a toothache.	Ha ga itamimasu.
I have a sore throat.	Nodo ga itamimasu.

[On A Telephone]

Hello.	Moshi, moshi.
May I speak to Mr.Yamada, please?	Yamada-san onegai-shimasu.
I'm Smith.	Smith desu.
What time do you expect him back?	Nanji ni modori-masu ka?
Please call me back.	Denwa o shite-kudasai.
I'll call you again.	Mata denwa o shimasu.

[Asking For Places Or Directions]

Where is a bathroom?	O-tearai wa doko desu ka?
Where is a poice box?	Kōban wa doko desu ka?
Where is a taxi stand?	TakushT-noriba wa doko desu ka?
Where is subway "Ginza Line"?	Chikatetsu "Ginza-Sen" wa doko desu ka?
Where is a public telephone?	Koshū-denwa wa doko desu ka?
On which floor do you sell umbrellas?	Kasa-uriba wa doko desu ka?
Is Tokyo Bank near here?	Tokyo-ginko wa kono chikaku desu ka?
Are there any gas stations near here?	Kono hen ni, gasorin-sutando arimasu ka?

[At A Station]

How much is the ticket to Shinjuku?	Shinjuku made ikura desu ka.
Will you tell me how to buy a ticket with this machine?	Kippu no kai-kata o oshiete-kudasai.
Small change, please.	Ryōgae onegai-shimasu.
One ticket to Kyoto.	Kyōto made, ichi-mai.
Two round-trip tickets to Nikko.	Nikkō made, ōhuku-kippu ni-mai.
By Special Express.	Tokkyū de.

By "Shinkan-sen."   Shinkan-sen de.

[At a Restaurant Or A Coffee Shop]
Will you give me a glass of water,
please?   Mizu onegai-shimasu.
Do you have a fixed menu?   Teishoku arimasu ka?
I'll eat deep-fried pork cutlet.   Tonkatsu onegai-shimasu.
I'll have coffee.   Kōhi kudasai.
Tea, please.   Kōcha kudasai.
Non-smoking seat, please.   Kin'en-seki onegai-shimasu.

[In A Taxi]
Please take me here. (Point and show
the address written on a piece of
paper.)   Koko made onegai-shimasu.
To IBM in Roppongi.   Roppongi no IBM made.
To Shiba Park Hotel.   Shiba Pāku Hoteru made.

[At A Store]
I'll take a 24-exposure film.   24(nijū-yon)mai-dori no huirumu o
                                     kudasai.
Do you accept traveller's checks?   Toraberā chekku tsukae-masu ka?
May I use a credit card?   Kurejitto-kādo tsukae-masu ka?
Show me this, please.   Kore o misete-kudasai.
I'll take this.   Kore o kudasai.
How much is it?   Ikura desu ka?

[At An Inn]
A room is available?   Heya arimasu ka?
I'd like to stay for two nights.   Huta-ban onegai-shimasu.
How much is it per night?   Ippaku ikura desu ka?
I'd like to check out.   Chekku-auto onegai-shimasu.

[At A Post Office]
Send it by air, please.   Kōkūbin de onegai-shimasu.
Send it by express, please.   Sokutatsu de onegai-shimasu.

Give me ten 100-yen stamps, please.   100(hyaku)en no kitte o jū-mai kudasai.
Three 70-yen stamps, please.   70(nanajū)en no kitte o san-mai.

Japanese-English Dictionary

A.	abiru	bathe
	abiseru	throw (water) on; rain (questions); lay (blame) on
	abuku	bubble; foam
	abura	oil; grease; fat
	aburae	oil painting
	achikochi	here and there; to and fro; back and forth
	achira	that; (over) there
	adana	nickname
	agaru	rise; go up; eat; drink

        ＊ <u>agaru</u> is the honorific form of <u>eat</u> and <u>drink</u>.

	agemono	fried food
	ageru	raise; lift; give

        ＊ <u>ageru</u> is the honorific form of <u>give</u>.

	ai	love; affection
	aida	space; interval; gap
	aidagara	relationship
	aijō	love; affection
	aikagi	duplicate key
	aikawarazu	still; as usual; as ever
	aikokushin	patriotism
	aikurushii	lovely; cute
	ainiku	unfortunately
	aisatsu	greeting; speech
	aishō	pet name
	aiseki suru	share a table
	aisu-kōhī	iced coffee
	aisu-kurīmu	ice cream
	ai suru	(v.) love
	aji	taste; flavor
	ajisai	hydrangea
	ajiwau	(v.) taste; experience
	aka	(n.) red
	akachan	baby
	akai	(adj.) red

akami	lean meat
akari	light; a light
akarui	light; bright
akeru	(v.) open
akeru	(v.) empty
aki	autumn
akiraka	clear; plain; evident
akirameru	give up
akireru	be disgusted with
akiru	be tired of
aku	become empty
aku	(v.) open
akubi	yawning
akusento	accent; emphasis
akushu o suru	shake hands
amadare	raindrop
amado	sliding shutter
amaeru	behave like a spoiled child
amagutsu	rain shoes
amai	sweet; sugary
amari	not very
amayakasu	indulge; coddle
amazake	sweet sake without alcohol
ame	rain
ame	candy
ami	net; netting
anata	you; my darling
	* anata is usually omitted, especially when addressing superiors, in which case the person's last name, title, or occupation is used if necessary.
ane	my elder sister
ani	my elder brother
anjiru	worry about; be anxious about
anki suru	learn by heart
anmin suru	sleep well
an´nai	(n.) guide; show

an´na ni	that much; in that way
an´nai suru	(v.) guide; show
ano	(attrib.) that; those
ansei	rest; repose
anshin suru	feel relieved; feel easy
anzen	safety; security
ao	(n.) blue
aoaza	bruise
aoi	(adj.) blue
aozameru	turn pale
apato	apartment; apartment building
ara	My goodness!; Why!
	* ara is a feminine expression.
arai	rough; coarse
arashi	storm
arasou	compete; argue; fight
arau	wash
are	that; that one
arekore	this and that
arerugī	allergy
ari	ant
arigatō	thanks
aruku	(v.) walk
arukōru	alcohol
asa	morning
asaban	mornings and evenings
asagao	morning glory
asagohan	breakfast
asahi	morning sun
asai	shallow
asatte	the day after tomorrow
ase	perspiration; sweat
ase o kaku	perspire; sweat
ashi	foot; leg; paw
ashikubi	ankle
ashita	tomorrow

asobu	play; amuse oneself
asu	tomorrow
ataeru	give; provide
atakamo	as if; just like
atamakin	down payment
atarashii	new; fresh; recent
atari	vicinity; the surroundings
ataru	hit; guess right
atatakai	warm; kind
atatamaru	warm oneself; get warm
atatameru	warm up; heat
atena	address written on an envelope
ato de	later; after
atsui	hot
atsukamashii	impudent
atsumaru	assemble; gather
atsumeru	gather; collect
atsuryoku	pressure
āu	fit; agree; match
āu	meet; encounter
awabi	abalone
ayamaru	apologize
ayashii	suspicious; queer; doubtful
ayu	sweetfish; ayu
azayaka(na)	vivid; splendid
B. ba	place; scene
bā	barroom
baai	case; situation; circumstances
bābekyū	barbecue
bāgen-sēru	bargain sale
bakkin	fine; penalty
baiten	stand; kiosk
baiu	rainy season
baka	(n.) fool; stupid (adj.) foolish; stupid
bakageta	silly; foolish

baketsu	pail; bucket
ban̄	evening; night
ban̄	one's turn
banchi	house number; street number
bango	number
bangumi	program
banzai	Long live the Emperor!; Hip, hip, hurray!
bara	rose
basho	place
basu	bus
batā	butter
batabata suru	bustle about
beddo	bed
Beikoku	America
bekkyo suru	live separately
bengoshi	lawyer
benkyō	(n.) study
benkyō suru	(v.) study
benri (na)	convenient
bentō	box lunch
bessō	villa; country house
betabeta suru	be sticky
betsu ni	separately
bi	beauty
bidanshi	handsome man
bideo	video
biiru	beer
bijin	beautiful woman (girl)
bijiness	business
bijutsu	art
bikkuri suru	be surprised at; be amazed at
bin	bottle
binsen	letter paper
biru	building
bishō suru	(v.) smile
bishonure ni naru	be soaked

bitamin	vitamin
biyōin	beauty parlor
biza	visa
bō	stick
bochi	graveyard; cemetery
bōchūzai	insect repellent
bōeki	trade; commerce
bōenkyō	telescope
bōhūu	rainstorm; typhoon
bokō	one's alma mater
bōkō	bladder
bokoku	one's country
bokokugo	mother tongue
boku	I

> *boku can be expressed by men in conversation with close
> people.

bon	tray
bōnenkai	year-end party
bonjin	ordinary person
bonsai	potted dwarf tree; bonsai
bonyarishita	dim; vague; absent-minded
boro	rags
bōshi	hat; cap
boshū suru	collect; raise; recruit
botan	button
bu	department; section; club
bubun	part; portion
budō	grapes
buenryo(na)	rude; impudent
buhin	parts; components
buji ni	safely; without accident
bukka	price of commodities
bukkyo	Buddhism
bun	sentence
bunbōgu	stationery
bungaku	literature

bunka	culture
bunkatsubarai	easy-payment
bunkō	branch school
bunmei	civilization
bunpo	grammar
bunrui suru	classify
bunryō	quantity
bunseki	analysis
bunsetsu	paragraph
bunshō	writing
bunsū	fraction
buntai	writing style
buntsū suru	correspond with
bunya	major field of interest
buranko	playground swing
burasagaru	hang; dangle
buta	pig; hog
butaniku	pork
butsurigaku	physics
buyō	dancing
byō	second
byō	thumbtack
byōbu	folding screen
byōin	hospital
byōki	illness; disease
byōreki	one's medical history

C.	cha	tea
	chadōgu	tea set
	chagashi	teacake; tea biscuit
	chairo	(n.) brown
	chairo(no)	(adj.) brown
	chakkarishita	shrewd; audacious
	chakuriku suru	make a landing
	chakuseki suru	sit down; be seated
	chan'neru	TV channel

chanoma	living room
chanoyu	tea ceremony
chanto	neatly; properly; punctually
chasaji	teaspoon
chawan	rice bowl; teacup
chi	blood
chibusa	breasts
chichi	my father
chigai	difference; distinction
chigau	differ; be wrong; disagree with
chihō	region
chiisai	small; very young
chijimaru	shrink
chijimeru	shorten; abridge
chijimu	shrink; contract
chijin	acquaintance
chikai	near
chikai	basement
chikamichi	shortcut
chikara	force; power; strength
chikarazuyoi	powerful; vigorous; encouraging
chikatetsu	subway
chikoku suru	be late
chippu	tip
chinpunkanpun	jargon; not understandable
chintai	(n.) lease
chirakaru	messy; be in disorder
chirakasu	mess up; scatter
chirashi	handbill; leaflet
chiri	dust
chiritori	dustpan
chiru	fall; be gone; scatter
chiryō suru	cure; treat
chishiki	knowledge
chiteki(na)	intellectual
chizu	map

chō	butterfly
chōchin	paper lantern
chōdai suru	receive; get
	* chodai suru is the humble form of receive.
chōdo	just; exactly
chōjo	eldest daughter
chōju	longevity
chōkan	morning paper
chōkanzu	bird´s-eye view
chokin	savings
chōkoku	sculpture
chokoreito	chocolate
chōkōsō	skyscraper
chōkōsei	auditor in classroom
chokuyaku	literal translation
chomei (na)	eminent; well-known
chōmiryō	seasoning
chōnan	eldest son
chōsa suru	investigate; examine
chōsen suru	challenge; defy
chosha	author
chōshi ga ii	feel well; be in good health
chōsho	strong point; merits
chōshoku	breakfast
chōshū	audience
chotto	for a short time
chūcho suru	hesitate
chūdan suru	discontinue; stop; interrupt
chūgakkō	junior high school
chūgakusei	junior high school student
chūgen	summer gift; midyear gift
chūjitsu (na)	faithful; loyal
chūko (no)	used; secondhand
chūkoku	advice; warning
chūmoku suru	pay attention
chūmon	(n.) order; request

chūō	center; middle
chūrippu	tulip
chūsha	injection
chūshajo	parking lot
chūshin	center
chūshoku	lunch; luncheon

D. **da**   am; are; is

         * <u>da</u> is the informal form of <u>desu</u>. Since it can sound
            abrupt, <u>da</u> is not usually used in woman's speech.

dabokushō	bruise
daeki	saliva
dai	title; heading
daibutsu	great image of Buddha
daidokoro	kitchen
daietto suru	(v.) diet
daigaku	college; university
daigakuin	graduate school; graduate course
daigishi	Dietman
daihyōsha	representative; delegate
daihyō suru	represent
daiji (na)	important; valuable
daijōbu	safe; secure; all right
daikin	charge; bill; fee
daikōbutsu	one's favorite food
daikon	Japanese radish
daiku	carpenter
daikyū	compensatory day off
dainashi ni suru	ruin; spoil
dairiseki	marble
dairiten	agency
daisū	algebra
daisuki (na)	favorite
daitai	about; almost
daitan (na)	bold; daring; undaunted
daitōryō	President

daiya	diamond
daizai	theme; subject
daizu	soybean
dakiageru	lift (a baby) in one's arms
dakishimeru	embrace tightly
daku	hold; hug
dame	no good; hopeless; impossible
danbō	heating
danchi	housing complex
dandan to	gradually; step by step
dangai	cliff
dango	dumplings
dangō suru	confer; consult
danjo	man and woman
danjo-kyōgaku	coeducation
dan'nen suru	give up; relinquish
danraku	paragraph
danro	fireplace; hearth
danryoku no aru	elastic; springy
dansei	male; man
danseiteki (na)	masculine; manly
danshi	boy; man
danshō suru	chat
dantei suru	conclude
dare	who
dareka	someone; anyone
darehitori	nobody
dasu	hold out; hand in; send
dāsu	dozen
datai	abortion
datsuzei	tax evasion
deau	come across
deguchi	exit
dekakeru	go out
dekigoto	incident; event
dekiru	be able to; be ready

dekitate no	fresh; just cooked
demo	but; and yet; still
demukaeru	go to meet (a person) at (an airport, a station, etc.)
denchi	battery
den'en	countryside
dengon	message
denki	electricity
denki	biography
denkyū	light bulb
denpō	telegram
denryū	electric current
densetsu	legend
densha	train; streetcar
dentō	electric light
dentōteki (na)	traditional
denwa	telephone
depāto	department store
deshi	disciple; pupil; apprentice
dēto o suru	make a date
dō	copper
dōbutsu	animal
dochira	where; who; which
dōgu	utensil; tool
dōhan suru	accompany
dōhu suru	enclose
dohyō	sumo ring
dōi	agreement; consent
dōigo	synonym
dōi suru	agree with; consent to
dōitsu no	identical; same
dōji ni	simultaneously
dōjitsu	the same day
dōjō	sympathy
dōjō suru	sympathize with
dokkairyoku	reading ability
dōki	motive

dokidoki suru	throb; palpitate
dōki ga suru	throb fast
dōkō	trend
doko	where
dokoka	somewhere
doku	poison
dokuritsu suru	be independent; stand alone
dokushin	single; unmarried
dokusōteki(na)	creative; unique
dōkyo suru	live together
dōkyūkai	class reunion
dōmo	hello; thank you; sorry
dōnattsu	doughnut
donburi	big bowl for soup or rice
don´na	what sort of
donogurai	how much; how many; how far; how long
dōon´igigo	homonym
doraibu suru	go for a ride
dore	which
doredemo	whichever; any one
doro	mud
dōro	road; street
dorobō	thief
doru	dollar
doryoku suru	make an effort; endeavor
dōsei	same sex
dōsei	same family name
dōsei suru	cohabit; live together
dōseki suru	share a table
dōshite	why; how
dōshitemo	by all means; just cannot
dōshokubutsu	animals and plants
dōsōsei	alumni
dōsōkai	alumni reunion
dōtoku	morality
dōwa	fairy tale; nursery story

dōyō	children's song; nursery rhyme
e	picture; painting; drawing
ē	yes; yeah; well
ebi	lobster; prawn; shrimp
echiketto	etiquette
eda	branch
Edokko	native Tokyoite
egao	smiling face
ehagaki	picture postcard
ehon	picture book
eibun	English sentence; English writing
eibungaku	English literature
eibun-wayaku	translation from English into Japanese
eiga	movie
eiga-haiyu	movie actor(actress)
eigakan	movie theatre
eigo	English language
eijū suru	reside permanently
eikaiwa	English conversation
eikō	glory
Eikoku	Britain
eikyō suru	influence; affect
eikyōryoku	influence
eiyaku	English translation
eiyo	honor; fame
eiyō no aru	nutritious
eiyōshi	deititian; nutritionist
eiyō-shicchō(no)	underfed
eiyū	hero
eizu	AIDS
eki	railroad station
ekichō	station master
ekiin	station employee
en	circle; yen
en	destiny; fate

endai	subject of a lecture(speech)
endan	marriage arrangements; marriage proposal
endō	roadside
engan	coast; shore
engeki	drama; theatre
enjo	assistance; support; help
enjuku	maturity; mellowness
enkai	banquet; feast
enki suru	postpone; adjourn
enman(na)	harmonious; amicable
en'nichi	temple(shrine) fair
enpitsu	pencil
enryo suru	be reserved; be modest
enryo no nai	unconstrained; frank
enryobukai	reserved; backward; modest
enseiteki(na)	pessimistic; misanthropic
ensō suru	perform; play
ensōkai	concert; recital
ensoku	excursion; outing
entotsu	chimney
enyūkai	garden party
enzetsu	public speech; address
enzetsu suru	make a speech; speak in public
erabu	choose; select
erai	great; extraordinary
eri	collar; neck
erimaki	muffler
eru	get; obtain; acquire
esa	bait; feed
ē to	well then
etsuran-shitsu	reading room
eyasui	easy to get; accessible

F.	fairu	(n.) file
	fakkusu	(n.) facsimile(fax)
	fasshon	fashion

fāsuto-hūdo	fast food
fesutebaru	festival
firumu	film
fōku	fork

G.
gai-jin	foreigner
gaiken	appearance
gaikoku	foreign country
gaikokugo	foreign language
gaikokujin	foreign person
gaikoku-kawase	foreign exchange
gairaigo	word of foreign origin
gairyaku	outline; summary
gaishoku suru	eat out
gaishutsu suru	go out
gaiyō	summary; synopsis
gaka	artist; painter
gake	cliff; precipice
gakka	subject of study; course of study
gakkai	academic society
gakkari suru	be disappointed
gakki	academic term; semester
gakki	musical instrument
gakkō	school; college
gakkō-kyōiku	shool education
gakubu	faculty; department
gakuchō	college president
gakudan	orchestra; band
gakuen	school; campus
gakugyō	studies; schoolwork
gakuhi	educational expenses
gakui	academic degree
gakumon	learning
gakunen	school year
gakureki	academic background
gakuryoku	scholastic ability

gakusei	student
gakusha	scholar; learned man
gakuwari	fare reduction for students
gaman suru	endure; bear with
gamanzuyoi	patient; forbearing
gamen	screen
gamu	chewing gum
ganbaru	persevere; bear up
ganjitsu	New Year's Day
gankai	eye doctor
gansho	application form
gantan	the first day of the year
gappi	date
garasu	glass; pane
garēji	garage
gasorin	gasoline
gasshuku suru	lodge together
gasu	gas
geijutsu	art
geijutsuka	artist
geka	surgery
gekai	surgeon
gekijō	theater ; playhouse
gekisakka	playwright; dramatist
gekiteki(na)	dramatic
gekkei	menstruation
gekkyū	monthly pay
gendai	modern times
gendaika	modernization
gengo	language
gengogaku	linguistics; philology
gen'in	(n.) cause
genjitsu ni	actually; practically
genjūsho	present address
genkaku(na)	strict; rigorous
genkan	front door; entrance

genki no ii	vigorous; lively
genkin	cash
genkō	manuscript; draft
genkotsu	fist
genkōyōshi	writing paper
genryō suru	reduce one's weight
genshoku	present post
genzō suru	develop negatives
gesha suru	get out of a car; get off the train
gessha	monthly tuition
gesshoku	lunar eclipse
gesshū	monthly income
geta	wooden clogs
getsuyōbi	Monday
gibo	mother-in-law
gidai	agenda
gihu	father-in-law
gikei	brother-in-law
gimu	duty; obligation
gimu-kyōiku	compulsory education
gin	silver
ginkō	bank
giron	argument; dispute
gisei	(n.) sacrifice
giseigo	onomatopoeia
gishi	engineer; technical expert
gishiki	ritual
go	five
gobai	five times
gobugobu	evenness; tie
gochagocha(no)	confused; mixed-up
gochisō	treat; feast
gogaku	language study; linguistics
gogatsu	May
gogo	afternoon
gohan	boiled rice; meal

goi	vocabulary
gojitsu	another day; future
gojū	fifty
gojūon	Japanese syllabary
gōka(na)	gorgeous; most luxurious
gokai suru	misunderstand
gōkaku suru	pass an examination; pass inspection
gōkei	total amount
Gokurō sama	Thank you for your trouble.
goma	sesame
gomakasu	cheat; deceive
gōman(na)	arrogant; proud
Gomen´nasai	Pardon me; Forgive me.
gomi	dust; rubbish
gomu	gum; rubber
goraku	pastime; pleasure
goruhu	golf
gōtō	burglar
gozen	a.m.
guai	condition; state
guragura suru	be shaky; be unsteady
gūzen ni	by chance; by accident
gyakutai suru	abuse; mistreat
gyō	line; row
gyōgi	manners; behavior
gyōji	event; function
gyokō	fishing port
gyōretsu suru	stand in line; line up
gyoson	fishing village
gyōza	Chinese dumpling
gyūniku	beef

H.

ha	tooth
ha	leaf
haburashi	toothbrush
hachi	eight

hachi	bee
hachigatsu	August
hachimitsu	honey
hada	skin
hadagi	underwear
hadaka	naked body; nudity
hadashi	bare feet
hae	(n.) fly
hagaki	postcard
hagemasu	encourage; spur on
hageshii	violent; passionate; strenuous
haguki	gums
haha	my mother
hai	lungs
hai	yes; no; certainly

> * Usage of hai is different from that of English yes
> and no. It is used to confirm either an affirmative
> or negative statement.

haiiro	gray; ashy
haikei	Dear Sir(or Madam); Gentlemen; Dear ...
haikingu	hiking
haiku	poem composed in groups of five, seven and five syllables
hairu	enter; join
haisha	dentist
haitatsu	delivery
haiyū	actor; actress
haizara	ashtray
hajimaru	begin; open
hajime	beginning; opening
Hajime mashite	How do you do?
hajimeru	begin; initiate
haka	grave; tomb
hakaru	measure; weight
hakike	nausea
hakken suru	discover; find
hakkiri	clearly; distinctly

hakko suru	publish; issue
hako	box; case
hakobu	carry; transport
hāku	vomit; throw up
hāku	put on (a skirt, pants, shoes, etc.)
hāku	sweep
hakuboku	chalk
hakubutsukan	museum
hakuchō	swan
hakujin	Caucasian
hakushigō	doctorate
hakushu	applause
hakushu o suru	clap one's hands
hamigaki	toothpaste
hamu	ham
han	seal; stamp
hanā	flower
hanā	nose
hanabi	fireworks
hanaji	nosebleed
hanami	picnic under cherry blossoms
hanamuko	bridegroom
hanareru	leave; separate
hanashi	talk; conversation
hanashiau	discuss
hanashizuki(na)	talkative; chatty
hanasu	talk; speak
hanayaka(na)	spectacular
hanayome	bride
hanbun	half
handan suru	judge; estimate; decide
handoru	steering wheel
hane	feather; wing
haneru	jump; leap; spring
hangaku	half the amount
hanga	woodblock print

han´igo	antonym
hankachi	handkerchief
hankagai	shopping quarters
hankōteki (na)	rebellious; defiant
han´nen	half a year
hansamu (na)	handsome
hansen	anti-war
hansū	half the number
hantai suru	oppose; object to
hantō	peninsula
hanzai	crime; offense
haori	short overgarment worn over a kimono
happyō suru	announce; make public
hara	stomach; abdomen
hara ga suku	get hungry
hara ga tatsu	get angry
harai-modosu	refund; pay back
harau	(v.) pay
hare	clear weather
hari	needle
haru	(n.) spring
harū	stick; paste
haru-yasumi	spring break
hasami	scissors
hashi	chopsticks
hashī	bridge
hashigo	ladder
hashiru	run; dash
hata	flag; banner
hatachi	twenty years of age
hatake	farm; field
hatarakimono	hard-working person
hataraku	work
hato	dove; pigeon
hatsuka	twenty days; the twentieth of a month
hatsumode	the first New Year's visit to a shrine or a temple

hatsuon	pronunciation
hatten suru	develop; expand
hayai	(adj.) fast; early
hayaku	(adv.) fast; early
hayashi	grove; woods
hazukashii	shameful; feel shy
hebi	snake
hei	fence; wall
heijitsu	weekday
heiki(na)	calm; cool
heikin	average; balance
heiten suru	close shop
heiwa	peace
henji	reply; response
henji suru	(v.) reply; answer
henken	prejudice; bias
hen(na)	odd; funny; peculiar
herasu	reduce; decrease
herikoputā	helicopter
heru	decrease; abate
heya	room
hī	day
hī	fire
hiatari no ii	sunny
hidari	left
hidarigawa	left side
hidoi	hard; unjust; outrageous
hieru	get chilly
hihu	skin
higashi	east
hige	mustache; beard
higeki	tragedy
higure	nightfall; dusk
hihanteki(na)	critical
hiimago	great-grandchild
hiji	elbow

hijōguchi	emergency exit; fire exit
hikage	shade
hikanronsha	pessimist
hikari	light; ray; flash
hikaru	shine; glitter
hikidashi	drawer
hikidasu	draw out from; bring out
hikinige	hit-and-run
hikiniku	ground meat
hikiukeru	undertake; accept
hikizan	subtraction
hikkoshi	house-moving
hikōki	airplane
hiku	pull; draw
hiku	play (a stringed instrument)
hiku	run over
hikui	low; short
hima ga aru	have time
hima o tsubusu	kill time
himitsu(no)	secret; confidential
himo	string; lace
Hinamatsuri	Doll Festival celebrated on March 3
hiniku	irony; sarcasm
hinode	sunrise
hinoiri	sunset
hinomaru	Rising-Sun flag (Japanese flag)
hinshitsu	quality
hiragana	Japanese cursive syllabary
hirō suru	announce; introduce
hiroba	square; plaza
hiroi	wide; broad
hirugohan	lunch
hiruma	day; daytime
hirune	nap; siesta
hiruyasumi	lunch break
hisashiburi ni	after a long time

hisho	private secretary
hisshū-kamoku	required subjects
hitai	forehead
hitei suru	deny; negate
hito	mankind; human being
hitoban	one night
hitori de	by oneself; for oneself
hitosashi-yubi	index finger
hitotsu	one; single
hitotsuki	one month
hitoyasumi suru	take a short break
hitsuyō(na)	necessary; inevitable
hiyake suru	get a tan; get sunburned
hiyasu	cool; refrigerate
hiyō	expenses; expenditure
hiza	knee; lap
hobo	nursery school teacher
hocchikisu	stapler
hōchō	kitchen knife
hodō	sidewalk
hodōkyō	pedestrian overpass
hoeru	bark; howl; roar
hōhu	aspiration; ambition
hōhu(na)	abundant; plentiful; affluent
hōgaku	direction
hogo suru	protect; shelter
hogosha	protector; guardian
hōhō	method; means
hohoemu	(v.) smile
hoikusho	daycare center
hojo	assistance; aid
hojokin	subsidy; grant
hoka no	other; another; different
hōkago	after school
hoken	insurance
hōkoku	report; briefing

hokori	dust
hokori'	pride
hokōsha	pedestrian
hōmen	direction
homeru	praise; admire
hōmon suru	visit; call on
hōmon-kyaku	visitor; caller
hōmuran	homerun hit
hon	book
hondana	bookshelf
hone	bone
honeyasume	relaxation
honmono	genuine article; real thing
hon´nō	instinct
honseki	one´s permanent domicile
honsha	head office of a firm
hontō(no)	true; actual; genuine
hontō ni	really
honya	bookstore
honyaku	translation
hoo	cheek
hora	boast; brag
Hora	Look!; There!
horaana	den; cave
horensō	spinach
horitsu	law
hoseki	jewel
hoshi	stars
hoshibudō	raisins
hoshii	want; would like to
hoshō suru	guarantee; warrant; assure
hoshuteki(na)	conservative
hosōdōro	paved street
hōsō	broadcasting
hosoi	thin; slim; narrow
hōsōkyoku	radio(TV) station

hōtai	bandage; dressing
hotaru	firefly
hoteru	hotel
huan	anxiety; uneasiness
huben (na)	inconvenient
hubo	father and mother
huchūi (na)	careless; imprudent
hude	writing brush; paintbrush
hudōsan	real estate
hueru	increase; breed
hūhu	married couple
hui ni	abruptly; suddenly
huirumu	film
hujin	woman
hujin	Mrs.
hujinka	gynecology
hukai	deep; profound; dense
hukai (na)	uncomfortable; unpleasant
hukaku	deeply; profoundly
hukanō (na)	impossible; impracticable
hukei	scenery; landscape
hukeizai (na)	uneconomical; wasteful
hukin	vicinity; neighborhood
huku	clothes; dress; suit
huku	wipe; mop
hukuro	bag; sack
hukushi	welfare
hukutsū	stomachache
hukyō	depression; recession
humikiri	railroad crossing
humoto	foot (of a mountain, hill, etc.)
humu	step on; trample on
hun	minute
hun	hmm; huh
hunabin de	by sea mail

hune	boat; ship
hun´iki	atmosphere
hunshitsu-butsu	lost article
hurahura	dizzily; unsteadily
hurai-pan	frying pan
hureru	touch; refer
huridasu	begin to rain(snow, hail, etc.)
hurisode	long-sleeved kimono
huro	bath
huroba	bathroom
huronto	front desk (of a hotel)
huroshiki	wrapping cloth
hurueru	tremble; shiver; shudder
hurugi	second-hand clothing
huruhon	used book
hurui	old; old-fashioned
hurusato	one´s home town
hurūtsu	fruits
husai	debt
hūsen	balloon
hūshū	custom; manners
husoku suru	be insufficient; be short
huta	lid; cover; cap
hutago	twins
hutan	burden; load
hutari	two persons
hutatabi	again
hutatsu	two
hūtō	envelope
hutoi	thick; fat; wide
huton	comforter; bedding
hutoru	gain weight
hutsū(no)	regular; ordinary; general
hutsuka	two days; the second day of a month
hutto suru	boil
huyasu	increase; raise

huyu	winter
huyuyasumi	winter vacation
huzai	absence
hyakka-jiten	encyclopedia
hyaku	one hundred
hyakubai	one hundred times
hyō	table; chart
hyō	(n.) vote
hyōban	reputation; popularity
hyōgen	expression; presentation
hyōjō	look; facial expression
hyōjun	standard; criterion; norm
hyōjungo	standard language
hyōka suru	evaluate; estimate
hyōronka	critic; commentator
hyōsatsu	doorplate
hyōshi	cover (of a book, a magazine, etc.)
hyōshiki	signpost
i	stomach
ibiki	snoring
icchi suru	accord with; coincide with
ichi	one
ichiba	market; fair
ichiban	best; most
ichiban	the first; No. 1
ichido	one time
ichigatsu	January
ichigo	strawberry
ichiji	one o'clock
ichijikan	for one hour
ichijiteki (na)	temporary; tentative
ichimai	one sheet (of paper); a copy (of photograph)
ichimei	one person
ichinen	one year
ichinensei	first-grade pupil; freshman

ichinichi	one day; whole day
ichiretsu	one line; one row
idai(na)	great; grand
ie	house; home
ihuku	clothes; apparel
igaku	medical science
igo	from now on; after that
ii	good; nice; fine
iiateru	guess right
iie	no; yes

       * Usage of <u>iie</u> is different from that of English
         <u>yes</u> and <u>no</u>. It is used to confirm either an
         affirmative or negative sentence.

iikaeru	say in other words
iikata	way of speaking; wording
iiko	good child
iimachigae	misstatement; slip of the tongue
iimono	good thing; goodies
iinaosu	rephrase; restate
iinchō	chairperson
iinkai	committee; board
iiowaru	finish speaking
iisugiru	say too much
iiwake o suru	make an excuse
ijimeru	tease; bully; peck at
ikaga	how; would you like; what about
ikari	anchor
ike	pond; reservoir
ikebana	flower arrangement
iken	opinion; idea; view
ikeru	can go; can find one's way to
iki	breath; respiration
ikigire ga suru	run out of breath
ikiiki to	lively; vividly
ikijibiki	walking dictionary
ikikata	way of life

ikikata	how to go to (a place)
iki no ii	fresh; lively
ikinokoru	survive
ikiru	(v.) live
ikisugiru	go too far; go to extremes
ikkagetsu	one month
ikkai	the first floor
ikoku	foreign country
iku	go; come (to see you)
ikudo	how many times; how often
ikudomo	many times; very often
ikuji no nai	weak; timid
ikujikan	how many hours; how long
ikujinashi	timid person; coward
ikunen	how many years
ikunichi	how many days; how long
ikunin	how many people
ikura	how much
ikutsu	how many; how old
īma	now; this day
ima	living room
imagoro	about this time; at this time
imamade ni	until now; by this time
imi	meaning
imin	immigration; emigration
imo	potato; sweet potato
imōto	one's younger sister
inabikari	lightning
inaka	the country; rural area
inakamono	hillbilly; country bumpkin
inemuri suru	(v.) doze
inhure	inflation
inkan	personal seal
inochi	life
inshōteki (na)	impressive; memorable
intai suru	retire; go into retirement

inu	dog
inyō suru	quote
ippai	one cup (of coffee); one glass (of water)
ippai ni naru	become full
ippaku suru	stop for the night; stay over the night
ippō	on the other hand
ippon	one piece (of chalk); one stick (of candy); one bottle (of beer)
ippun	one minute
iraira suru	become irritated; lose patience
Irasshai	Come in; Welcome.
irrasharu	come; go; be
	* irrasharu is the honorific form of come, go and be.
ireru	put in; admit; include
iriguchi	entrance; gate
iritamago	scrambled eggs
iro	color
iroiro(na)	various; diverse
iru	be; exist; there is(are)
	* iru is used only for the animate.
iru	need; want; require
irui	clothing; garments
iseki	ruins
isha	physician; doctor
ishi	stone; pebble
ishi	physician; doctor
ishi no tsuyoi	strong-willed
ishokujū	food, clothing and shelter
isogashii	busy
isogu	hasten; hurry
isoide	in haste; in a hurry
issakujitsu	day before yesterday
issakunen	year before last year
issho ni	together
isshōkenmei ni	with all one's might; very hard
isshūkan	for one week

isu	chair; couch
itadaku	have; receive; eat; drink
	* <u>itadaku</u> is the humble form of <u>have</u>, <u>receive</u>, <u>eat</u>, <u>drink</u>, etc.
itai	painful
itamae	cook at a Japanese restaurant
itami	pain; ache
itamu	hurt; ache; have a pain
iten suru	move; change one's residence
itoko	cousin
itsu	when; what time; how soon
itsudemo	any time; any day
it͞suka	five days; the fifth day of a month
˥itsuka	some day; in time; one day
itsumade	how long; till when
itsumo	always; all the time
itsutsu	five; five years old
Itte kimasu	I'll go and come back.
Itte rasshai	Please go and come back.
	* The above two are set expressions. The former is said when leaving home while the latter is an automatic response.
iu	say; utter; remark; tell
iwai	celebration
iwau	congratulate; celebrate
iya(na)	unpleasant; disgusting
iya ni naru	become tired of; feel repugnance to
iyokuteki ni	enthusiastically
izakaya	tavern; pub
J. jagaimo	potato
jakuten	weakness; disadvantage
jama suru	interfere; disturb
jamu	jam
jazu	jazz
jibiki	dictionary

Jibun	self; oneself
Jidai	era; period; age
Jiden	autobiography
Jidō-hanbaiki	automatic vending machine
Jidōsha	automobile
Jigazō	self-portrait
Jigyō	enterprise; business
Jihatsuteki ni	spontaneously; voluntarily
Jihibukai	merciful; compassionate
Jijitsu	fact; truth
Jijō	circumstances; conditions
Jikaku suru	be aware of; realize
Jikan	hour; time
Jikandōri ni	punctually; on schedule
Jikanhyō	timetable
Jikan ni okureru	be late for
Jikken	experiment; test
Jikkō suru	practice; execute; carry out
Jikkuri to	thoroughly; without haste
Jiko	accident
Jikoku	time; hour
Jiko-shōkai	self-introduction
Jiman suru	be boastful
Jimejimeshita	damp; humid
Jimu	office work
Jimuin	clerk; office worker
Jimusho	office; one's place of business
Jimuteki (na)	businesslike; practical
Jinbungaku	humanities
Jinja	Shinto shrine
Jinkō	population
Jinruigaku	anthropology
Jinseikan	one's view of life
Jinshu	race
Jinshu-sabetsu	racial discrimination
Jiritsu suru	become independent

Jirojiro miru	stare at
Jisa	difference in time
Jisaboke	jet lag
Jishin no aru	confident
Jishin	earthquake
Jisho	dictionary
Jissai wa	to tell the truth; in fact
Jitaku	one's own house; one's home
Jitensha	bicycle
Jitsugyōka	businessman
Jitsurei o ageru	give an example
Jitsu wa	the fact is ....
Jitsuyōteki (na)	practical
Jitto miru	stare at
Jiyū	freedom; liberty
Jizen	charity; philanthropy
Jōdan	joke; jest
Jogen	advice; suggestion
Jogen suru	advise; suggest
Jōhin (na)	refined; dainty
Jōhō	information; intelligence
Joseito	schoolgirl
Jōken	conditions
Jōkigen de	in a merry mood; in high spirits
Jōkyaku	passenger
Jokyōju	assistant professor; associate professor
Jōkyū	advanced course
Jōkyūsei	upper-class student; senior student
Jōnetsuteki (na)	passionate; ardent
Jōō	queen
Jōryū-shakai	upper classes; high society
Josei	woman
Joseiteki (na)	womanly; feminine
Jōshaken	railroad (bus) ticket
Joshi	woman; girl; female
Jōshiki	common sense; common knowledge

jōshikiteki (na)	sensible
Joshu	assistant
jōyaku	treaty
joyū	actress
jōzu (na)	skillful; dexterous
jū	ten
jūbun (na)	enough; sufficient
jūbun ni	sufficiently; fully
jūdō	<u>Judo</u>: Japanese martial art
jūgatsu	October
jugyō	class; session
jugyōryō	tuition
jūichigatsu	November
jūjiro	crossroads
juken suru	take an examination
juku	cram school
jukugo	idiomatic phrase; idiom
jūmin	inhabitants; residents
junbi	preparation
junbi suru	prepare; make ready
jūnen	ten years
jūnigatsu	December
junkyū	semi-express train
junsa	police officer; patrolman
junsui (na)	pure; genuine
jūsho	address; one's dwelling place
jūshoroku	address book
jūsu	juice
jūtaku	house; residence
jūtan	carpet; rug
juwaki	telephone receiver
jūyō (na)	important
ka	mosquito
kaban	bag; satchel; briefcase
kabe	wall

kabin	flower vase
kabocha	pumpkin; squash
kabu	turnip
kabuki	Japanese traditional drama
kaburu	put on (a hat); pour (water) on oneself
kachi	value; worth
kachi no aru	valuable; worthy
kado	corner; edge
kadō	flower arrangement
kādo	card; credit card
kadomatsu	New Year´s gate decorations usually made of pine, bamboo and plum
kaerigake ni	on one´s way back home; on one´s leaving
kaeru	frog
kaeru	return; go(come) back ~~home~~
kaeru	exchange; substitute
kaesu	give back; return
kagai-katsudō	extracurricular activities
kagaku	science
kagami	mirror; looking glass
kage	shade
kagen ga warui	feel ill
kagi	key; hook
kago	cage; basket
kagu	(v.) smell; scent; sniff
kahunshō	hay fever; pollen allergy
kai	shellfish; shell
kaichō	president; chairperson
kaichū-dentō	flashlight
kaidan	conference; meeting
kaidan	staircase; steps
kaigai e iku	go abroad
kaigai-ryokō	travelling abroad
kaigan	seashore; seacoast
kaigi	conference; meeting
kaigō	meeting; assembly; get-together

kaihatsu suru	develop
kaihi	membership fee
kaijō	upper floor
kaika	lower floor
kaikai suru	open a meeting
kaikatsu(na)	cheerful; lively
kaikei-gakari	cashier; accountant
kaiketsu suru	solve; settle
kaimono	shopping
kaimono ni iku	go shopping
kairyō suru	improve; reform
kaisai suru	hold (a conference); open (an exhibition)
kaisatsu-guchi	ticket gate
kaisha	company
kaishain	company employee; office worker
kaishō suru	cancel
kaisō suru	recall; recollect
kaisō	seaweed
kaisoku-densha	rapid train
kaisuiyoku	sea bathing
kaitō-yōshi	answer sheet
kaiwa	conversation; talk
kaizen suru	improve; better
kaji	a fire
kaji o suru	do housework; keep house
kajiru	bite; gnaw; nibble at
kakaeru	carry (a thing, a person) under one's arm
kakari	person in charge; clerk in charge
kakaru	take; need; cost
kakato	heel
kakawarazu	though; although; in spite of
kake-buton	bedspread; covers
kakegae no nai	irreplaceable; precious (life, person, etc.)
kakegoto	bet; gambling
kakeru	hang; sit down; sprinkle over; spend (money, time)
kakezan	multiplication

kaki	oyster
kaki	persimmon
kaki-atsumeru	rake up; gather up
kakigōri	shaved ice; slush (sweets)
kakine	hedge; fence
kakitome	registered mail
kakko ii	stylish; well-proportioned
kakoku (na)	harsh; cruel; merciless
kaku	write; compose; draw; paint
kaku	scratch
kakudaikyō	magnifying glass
kakudo	angle
kakueki ni tomaru	stop at every station
kakugetsu	every other month
kakujitsu (na)	certain; reliable
kakujitsu ni	surely; certainly
kakunin suru	confirm; affirm; identify
kakureru	hide; conceal oneself
kakushin suru	be convinced of; be sure of
kakushū	every other week
kakusu	hide; conceal
kamaboko	boiled fishcake
kame	tortoise; turtle
kamera	camera
kami	paper
kami-bukuro	paper bag
kaminari	thunder
kami no ke	hair of the head
kamisori	razor
kamoku	subjects; curriculum
kamome	sea gull
kamu	bite; crunch; chew
kanarazu	certainly; surely; without fail
kanari	fairly; pretty; considerably
kanashii	sad; sorrowful; mournful
kanashimu	be grieved at; feel sad about

kanban	signboard; billboard
kandai (na)	generous; tolerant
kandō suru	be impressed by; be moved by
kane	metal; money
kane	bell; chime
kanemochi	rich person
kangae	thought; idea
kangaeru	think; consider; imagine
kangeikai	welcome reception
kangei suru	welcome
kangohu	nurse
kango suru	nurse; look after
kani	crab
kanja	(n.) patient
kanji	Chinese character used in Japanese writing
kanji no ii	agreeable
kanjiru	feel; be sensitive to
kanjō	feelings; emotion
kanjōteki (na)	emotional
kanjōteki ni naru	get emotional
kankei	relationship; connection
kankei ga aru	be related to; be relevant to
kankō	sight-seeing
kankō ni iku	go sight-seeing; do the sights of
kankō-kyaku	tourist
kankō-ryokō	sight-seeing tour
kankyō	environment; circumstances
kanojo	she; girlfriend
kanōsei	possibility; potentiality
kanpai suru	make a toast to
kanpeki (na)	perfect; impeccable
kansatsu suru	observe; view
kansei suru	complete; finish up
kansei o ageru	shout for joy; give a cheer
kansha suru	thank; express one's gratitude; be grateful for

kanshin o motsu	be concerned about; be interested in
kanshō suru	interfere; meddle
kanshoku	(n.) touch; feel
kanshōteki (na)	sentimental; emotional
kanshū	custom;convention; common practice
kanshū	spectator; audience
kantan (na)	simple; brief
kantoku suru	supervise; direct
kanyōgo	idiom
kanyō (na)	generous
kanzei	custom duty; tariff
kanzen ni	perfectly; thoroughly
kanzume	canned goods
kao	face
kaoiro	complexion
kaori	fragrance; perfume
kaoru	be fragrant; smell
kappatsu (na)	active; lively; spirited
karada	body; health
karada ni ii	be good for the health
karada ni warui	be bad for the health
karai	hot; spicy
karakau	tease; make fun of
kara (no)	empty; vacant
karaoke	recorded music followed by singing
karashi	mustard
karasu	crow; raven
karate	self-defense art
kare	he; boyfriend
karendā	calendar
karē-raisu	curry and rice
kariru	borrow; rent
karōshi	death from overwork
karui	(adj.) light
kasen o hiku	(v.) underline
kashi	confectionery

kashikoi	wise; intelligent
kashi-shitsu	room-for-rent; apartment-for-rent
kashu	singer
kassai	applause; acclamation
kasu	(v.) loan; rent
kata	shoulder
katachi	form; shape; figure
kata ga koru	have a stiff-shoulder
katai	hard; solid
katamichi-jōshaken	one-way ticket
katamichi-ryōkin	one-way fare
katana	sword
katarogu	catalogue
katazukeru	tidy up; clean up
katei	home; household
katei-kyōshi	tutor
kāten	curtain; drapes
katorikku-kyōkai	Catholic church
katsu	win
katsujitai de kaku	print; write in block letters
kau	buy; purchase
kawari-yasui	changeable; unsettled
kawaru	change
kawase	money order
kawase-sōba	exchange rate
kawatta	different; unusual
kayou	commute
kayui	itchy
kazan	volcano
kazaru	ornament
kaze	wind; breeze
kaze o hiku	catch cold
kazoeru	count; number
kazoku	family
kazu	number
kega	injury; wound

kega o suru	get hurt; be injured; be wounded
kegawa	fur
keibatsu	punishment; penalty
keibetsu suru	despise; disdain
keiei suru	manage; operate
keihi	expenses
keijiban	bulletin board
keikaku	plan; project
keikaku o tateru	make a plan
keikan	police officer
keiken	(n.) experience
keiken suru	(v.) experience
keiko	practice; training
keikoku suru	warn; caution; admonish
keireki	one's background
keiri	accounting
keisan	calculation
keisanki	calculator
keisatsu	police force
keisatsukan	police officer
keisatsusho	police station
keishoku	light meal; snack
keiyaku	contract; agreement
keiyaku o musubu	make a contract with; make an agreement with
keiyu suru	go via; go through
keizai	economy
keizaigaku	economics
keizaiteki (na)	economical
kēki	cake
kekka	result; consequence
kekkō (na)	good; fine; right
kekkon	marriage
kekkon-shiki	wedding ceremony
kekkon suru	marry; get married to
kekkyoku	after all; eventually; finally
kemuri	(n.) smoke

ken	prefecture
kenbutsunin	spectator
kenbutsu suru	sight-see
kenchikuka	architect
kendō	Japanese swordsmanship
kenka	quarrel; fight
kenkai	opinion; view
kenka suru	have a quarrel with; fight
kenkō(na)	healthy; sound
kenkō-hokenshō	health insurance card
kenkō-shindan	medical examination
kenkyū	study; research
kenmei ni	hard; earnestly
kenpō	constitution
kenryoku no aru	powerful; influential
kensa suru	inspect; examine
kensetsu suru	construct
kenson suru	be modest
kentō ga tsukanai	have no idea of
kenyaku suru	be frugal; economize
keredomo	but; however
kesa	this morning
keshigomu	rubber eraser
keshiki	scenery; landscape
keshōhin	cosmetics
keshōshitsu	restroom; powder room
kessaku	masterpiece
kesseki suru	be absent from; fail to attend
kesshin	determination; resolution
kesshin suru	determine; make up one's mind
ketsuatsu	blood pressure
ketsueki	blood
ketsuron o dasu	come to a conclusion
ketten	weak point; defect
ki	tree; shrub; wood
kibishii	severe; strict

kibō	hope; wish; aspiration
kibun ga ii	feel good
kichigai-jimita	crazy; mad; lunatic
kichi ni tomu	be witty; be full of resources
kichin to shita	neat; tidy
kichōhin	valuables
kiga	hunger; starvation
kihu	contribution; donation
ki ga au	get along well
kigae	change of clothes
ki ga tsuku	realize
kigen ga ii	be in a good mood
kigu	appliance
kihonteki(na)	fundamental; basic
kiiro	(n.) yellow
kiji	news item; article
kikai	machine
kikai	opportunity
kikai ga attara	if given a chance
kikaku	planning; plan
kiken(na)	dangerous
kikinikui	difficult to hear
kikitore nai	be inaudible
kikō	climate
kikoeru	can hear; be audible
kikonsha	married person
kiku	chrysanthemum
kiku	hear; listen to
kimeru	decide
kimochi ga ii	feel good
kimochi ga warui	feel sick
kimyō(na)	strange; odd
kin	gold
kinben(na)	industrious
kinchō suru	become tense
kindaika	modernization

Kin´en	No Smoking.
kinenbi	memorial day; commemoration day
kingaku	amount of money
ki ni iru	like; be pleased
ki ni suru	worry; mind; care
kinjo	neighborhood
kinko	safe; cashbox
kinkō	suburbs; outskirts
kinkyū(no)	urgent
kinō	yesterday
kinoko	mushroom
kinu	silk
kinyōbi	Friday
kioku suru	remember; memorize
ki o tsukeru	be careful of; watch out
kippu	ticket
kippu-uriba	ticket office; box office
kirai(na)	distasteful; disagreeable
kiraku(na)	carefree; easy
kirei(na)	beautiful; pretty; clean
kiri	mist; fog
kīru	cut; chop
kiru	put on; wear
kisaku(na)	frank; open-hearted
kisekiteki(na)	miraculous
kisetsu	season
kisha	newspaperman; journalist
kishō	weather conditions
kishukusha	boarding house; dormitory
kisoku	rule; regulations
kissaten	coffee shop; cafe
kita	north
kitai suru	expect; hope for
kitai-hazure(no)	disappointing
kitaku suru	return home
kitanai	dirty; filthy

kitsune	fox
kitte	postage stamp
kitto	surely; certainly
kizetsu suru	faint; lose consciousness
kizuku	take notice of
kō	like this; in this way
kōjō	factory
kōban	police box
kobosu	(v.) spill
kobushi	fist
kōbutsu	one's favorite dish
kōcha	black tea
kochira	this place; here; this side; this way
kōchō	principal; headmaster
kōdōteki (na)	active; aggressive
kōdō	auditorium
kodoku (na)	lonely; solitary
kōdoku suru	subscribe
kodomo	child
koe	voice
kōen	park; public garden
kōhuku (na)	happy; blessed
kōhun suru	get excited
kōgai	environmental pollution
kōgai	suburbs; outskirts
kōgeki suru	attack
kōgi	(n.) protest
kōgi	(n.) lecture
kogitte	(n.) check
kogitte o kiru	write out a check
kogu	row
kōgyō	manufacturing industry
kōhai	younger generation; one's junior
kōhi	coffee
kōhosha	candidate; applicant
koi	(n.) love

koi	carp
koibito	lover; boyfriend; girlfriend
koinobori	carp-shaped streamers flown on Children's Day, or the Boy's Festival, on May 5th
koishi	pebble
kojiki	beggar; tramp
kojin(no)	individual; personal; private
kōjitsu o tsukuru	make an excuse
kōka	coin
kōkan suru	make an exchange
kōkishin	curiosity; inquisitiveness
kōkishin no tsuyoi	curious; inquisitive
kokka	country; nation; state
kokka	national anthem
kokkai	Diet
kokki	national flag
kokku	(n.) cook
koko	here; this place
kōkō	senior high school
kokochi ii	comfortable; cozy
kōkoku	advertisement
kokoro	spirit; heart; mind
kokoro kara	from the heart
kōkōsei	senior high-school student
kōkūbin	airmail
kōkū-gaisha	airline company
kokugo	Japanese language; one's mother tongue
kokuhō	national treasure
kōkūken	airline ticket
kokumin no shukujitsu	national holiday
Kokuren	U.N.
kokuritsu-daigaku	national university
kokuritsu-kōen	national park
kokusai-denwa	international telephone
kokusai-kōryū	international cultural exchange
kokusai-kyōryoku	international cooperation

kokuseki	nationality; citizenship
kōkū-yūbin	airmail
kokyō	one's hometown; one's birth place
Kōkyo	Imperial Palace
kokyū suru	breathe
komaru	be distressed by; be in trouble
komatta	troubled
kome	rice
kōmon	school gate
komori	baby-sitter
kōmorigasa	umbrella
kōmuin	public official; govenment employee
kona	flour; powder
Konbanwa	Good evening.
kondate	menu; bill of fare
kondo	this time; next time
kongetsu	this month
konimotsu	parcel; package
konkai	this time
konkiyoku	patiently; persistently
kon'nan	difficulty
Kon'nichiwa	Good afternoon; Good day; Hello.
konoaida	the other day; a short time ago
konogoro	these days; nowadays
konoha	leaves of trees
konohen	this neighborhood
konokata	this person
konotsugi	next
konshū	this week
konya	this evening; tonight
konyaku suru	be engaged to
kopī o toru	make a copy; duplicate
koppu	glass
kore	this; this one
korekara	from now on; in the future
koremade	until now; up to here

kōri	ice
kōritsu-gakkō	public school
korosu	kill
kōryo suru	consider; think over
kosame	light rain; drizzling rain
kōsaten	crossing; intersection
kōsei-busshitsu	antibiotic
koshi	waist; hips
koshi o kakeru	sit down
koshō	pepper
Koshōchu	Out of Order.
kōshū-denwa	public telephone; pay phone
kōshū-yokujō	public bathhouse
kōsō-kenchiku	skyscraper
kōsoku-dōro	expressway; turnpike; freeway
kosuru	rub; scrape
kotae	(n.) answer; reply
kotaeru	(v.) answer; reply
koto	traditional Japanese harp with thirteen strings
kotoba	language; speech; word
kōtō-gakkō	senior high school
kotori	small bird
kotoshi	this year
kotowaru	refuse; reject
kotowaza	proverb; saying
kotozuke	message
kōtsū	traffic
kōtsūihan	violation of traffic regulations
kōtsūjiko	traffic accident
kōtsū-kisoku	traffic rules
kōtsū-shingō	traffic signal
kowai	fearful; scary
kowareru	be broken; get out of order
kōza	account
kozeni	small change
kozukai	pocket money; allowance

kozutsumi	parcel; package
kū	nine
kū	ward; borough
kubi	neck
kuchi	mouth
kuchibiru	lips
kudamono	fruit
kudari-zaka	downhill
kugatsu	September
kugi	nail
kuji	lottery; raffle
kūki	air
kūkō	airport
kumo	clouds
kumo	spider
kumoru	become cloudy
kuni	country; nation
kuraberu	compare; make a comparison
kurai	dark; gloomy
kuraku naru	get dark
kurejitto-kādo	credit card
kurikaesu	repeat
Kurisumasu	Christmas Day
kuro	(n.) black
kuroi	black; dark
kuru	come
kuruma	automobile; car
kurumaisu	wheelchair
kurushii	painful; afflicting
kurushimu	suffer; agonize
kusa	grass; weed
kusaru	rot; spoil; decay
kūseki	vacant seat
kushami	sneezing
kushi	comb
kusuri	medicine; drug

kusuriya	pharmacy; drugstore
kutabireru	get tired; be fatigued
kutsu	shoes; boots
kutsushita	socks; stockings; panty hose
kutsuya	shoe store
kuwaeru	add
kuwashii	detailed
kuzukago	wastebasket
kyabetsu	cabbage
kyaku	visitor; guest; customer
kyō	today
kyōchō suru	emphasize; stress
kyōdai	sibling
kyōiku	education
kyōikugaku	pedagogy
kyōikuhi	educational expenses
kyōikuteki (na)	educational
kyōin	teaching staff
kyōin-menkyo	teaching certificate
kyōju	teaching; instruction; professor
kyoka	permission; approval
kyōkai	church
kyōkasho	school textbook
kyoku	tune; melody
kyōmibukai	very interesting
kyōmi o motsu	be interested in
kyonen	last year
kyori	distance
kyōryoku suru	cooperate with; collaborate with
kyōseiteki (na)	compulsory
kyōshi	teacher; instructor
kyōshitsu	classroom; lecture room
kyōsō	competition; contest; race
kyōsō-aite	rival; competitor
kyōzai	teaching materials
kyū	nine

kyūjitsu	holiday
kyūka	holidays; vacation; sabbatical
kyūka o toru	take a vacation; get a leave of absence
kyūkei suru	take a break
kyūkei-jikan	recess; intermission
kyūkō-densha	express train
kyū ni	suddenly; unexpectedly
kyūri	cucumber
kyūryō	pay; wages; salary
kyūryōbi	pay day
kyūsoku	rest; relaxation
kyūyō	urgent business
mabushii	glaring; dazzling
machi	town; city
machiai-shitsu	waiting room
machigaeru	make a mistake
machigai	error; mistake
mada	not yet; still
made	till; until; up to
mado	window
mae	front; ago
maemotte	beforehand; in advance
magarikado	street corner
magaru	bend; make a turn
mago	grandchild
maguro	tuna
mahōbin	thermos bottle
maiasa	every morning
maiban	every evening
maigetsu	every month
maikai	every time
mainen	every year
mainichi	every day
maishū	every week
majime(na)	serious

makaseru	leave (a matter) to (a person); entrust (a person) with (a task)
makura	pillow
mame	beans; peas
mamemaki	bean-throwing ceremony held on Febuary 3rd or 4th
mamonaku	soon
mamoru	protect; defend
man	ten thousand
manabu	learn
manbiki	shoplifting
manga	comic strip; cartoon
man´ichi no baai niwa	in case of emergency
manjū	bun with bean-jam inside
mankai ni naru	come into full bloom
man´naka ni	just in the middle of; right in the center
manpuku	full stomach
manzoku(na)	satisfactory
manzoku suru	be satisfied with
Masaka	Impossible!
massugu(na)	straight; erect; honest
mata	again
mataseru	keep (a person) waiting
matsu	pine tree
matsu	wait; await
matsu-kazari	New Year´s pine decorations
matsuri	festival
mattaku	entirely; thoroughly
mawari-michi	(n.) detour
mawaru	turn around; revolve
mayonaka	midnight
mayou	lose one´s way
mazeru	mix; mingle
mazu	first of all
me	eye
medama-yaki	sunny-side up
megane	glasses; spectacles

me ga warui	have an eye disease; have bad eyesight
megumi	blessing; mercy; charity
megusuri	eyewash; eye lotion
mei	niece
meibutsu	noted product; special product
meimonkō	prestigious school
me o tōsu	scan
meirei	order; command
meishi	calling card; name card
meisho-kyūseki	scenic spots and places of historic interest
mejirushi	landmark
memai	dizziness
men	cotton
mendō o kakeru	give (a person) trouble
mendō o miru	take care; look after
menjō	diploma; certificate
menkyoshō	license; certificate
menrui	noodles; vermicelli
mensetsu	interview
me o samasu	wake up; awake
meshiagaru	eat; drink
	* meshiagaru is the honorific expression of eat and drink
metta ni	rarely; seldom
mezamashi-dokei	alarm clock
mezurashii	unusual; rare
miageru	look up; raise one´s eyes
miai	arranged marriage-meeting
mibōjin	widow
mibun-shōmeisho	identification card
michi	road; street
michi o kiku	ask direction to
midashi	index; caption; headline
midori	green; verdure
mieru	able to see; be visible; look
migi	(n.) right

Migigawa tsūkō	Keep to the right.
migoto(na)	beautiful; superb; skillful
mihon	sample; model
mijikai	short; brief
mikan	mandarin orange; tangerine
mikata	viewpoint
mikka	three days; the third day of a month
mikomi ga aru	be hopeful; have a bright future
mikoshi	portable shrine
mimawasu	look around; make a survey
mimi	ear; hearing
mina	all; everything; everybody
minami	south
minasan	all of you; everybody, ladies and gentlemen
minato	harbor; port
mingeihin	folkcrafts
minikui	ugly; mean
minshuku	Bed & Breakfast
minzoku	ethnos; race
miokuru	see (a person) off
mirai	future
miru	see; look; observe
miruku	milk
miryokuteki(na)	charming; attractive
mise	store; shop
miseinensha	person under age; minor
miseru	show; exhibit
miso	soybean paste used as seasoning
mitsu	honey; nectar
mitsukeru	find out; discover
miyage	souvenir
miyasui	easy to see
mizu	water
mizugi	swimming suit
mizuumi	lake
mō	already; yet; another; more

mō hitori	one more person; another person
mō hitotsu	one more(thing)
mochi	rice cake
mochidasu	carry out; take out
mochi-kaeru	carry back
mochikomu	carry in; take to
mochinushi	owner
mochiron	of course
modoru	return; go(come) back
moeru	burn; be in flames
mohō	imitation
moji	letter; character
mōjin	blind person
mokuhanga	wood-block print
mokuji	table of contents
mokuteki	purpose; aim
mokutekichi	destination; goal
momen	cotton; cotton cloth
mōmo	thigh
momō	peach; peach tree
mon	gate
Monbushō	Ministry of Education
mondai	question; problem
monku o iu	complain
mono	thing; object
monogatari	story; tale
monosashi	measuring rule; scale
monosugoi	horrible; awful
morau	get; receive
mori	woods; forest
moroi	fragile
motsu	have; hold
motte-kaeru	bring(take) back
motte-kuru	bring; fetch
motte-iku	take; carry away
motto	more; longer

mudazukai o suru	(v.) waste
mugi	barley; wheat; oats; rye
muika	six days; the sixth day of a month
mujaki(na)	innocent
mukae ni iku	go for (a person)
mukai ni	on the opposite side
mukanshin	indifference
mukashi	old times; old days
muko	bridegroom; son-in-law
mukōgawa	opposite side
muku	turn; turn one's face
mune	chest
mura	village
murasaki	purple
muryō de	for free; without charge
mushi	insect; worm
mushi suru	ignore; neglect
mushiba	decayed tooth
musubu	tie; fasten
musuko	son
musume	daughter; young woman
mutsumajii	intimate; affectionate
muttsu	six
muzukashii	hard; difficult
myaku	pulse; hope
myō(na)	strange; odd
myōgonichi	day after tomorrow
myōji	family name
myōnichi	tomorrow

N.	nabe	pan; pot
	nagagutsu	boots
	nagai	(adj.) long
	nagaisu	sofa; couch
	nagaku	for a long time; forever
	nagame	view; outlook

nagameru	look on; gaze at
nagasa	length
nagashi	(n.) sink
nagasode	long sleeves
naga-zubon	long trousers
nageru	throw; pitch
nagori-oshii	be reluctant to leave; feel the sorrow of parting
nagusameru	comfort; console
nahuda	name tag; nameplate
nai	there is no; do not have; be out of
naihu	knife
naisen-bangō	extension number
naishinsho	school report
naisho-banashi	confidential talk
nakama	company; comrade
nakayoku suru	make friends; get along well
nakōdo	matchmaker
naku	cry; weep
nama	raw; uncooked
namae	name
namakemono	lazy fellow
namakeru	be lazy
nama-tamago	raw egg
nameraka(na)	smooth; velvety
nami	wave; surf
namida	(n.) tear
nana	seven
nanatsu	seven
nanban	what number
nandemo	anything; whatever
nando	how many times; how many degrees
nani	what
nanika	something; anything
nanimo	nothing
naniyōbi	what day of the week
nanji	what time

nanjikan	how many hours
nan'nen	how many years; what year
nan'nensei	what grade(year)
nan'nichi	how many days; what day
nan'nin	how many people
nansai	how old; what age
nantoka	anyhow; somehow
naoru	be repaired; be mended
naoru	get well; recover; be cured
naosu	mend; correct
naosu	cure; heal
napukin	napkin
narabu	stand in line; line up
narau	learn; practice
nareru	get used to; become accustomed to
naru	become; come to (do); play the role of; get (dark)
narubeku	if circumstances allow
naruhodo	I see; indeed
nashi	pear
nashitogeru	accomplish; achieve
nasu	eggplant
natsu	summer
natsukashii	long for; feel homesick for
natsu-yasumi	summer vacation
nattō	fermented soybeans
nawatobi	rope skipping
naze	why
ne	root
nebiki	discount
nebō suru	oversleep
nedan	price; cost
nedan ga takai	be expensive
nadan ga yasui	be inexpensive
negau	(v.) wish; desire; hope
negokochi no ii	comfortable to sleep
nekkuresu	necklace

neko	cat
nekutai	necktie
nemaki	nightgown; pajamas
nemui	sleepy
nemuru	sleep; fall asleep
nēndo	year; term
nēndo	clay
nengajō	New Year's card
nen-ga-ppi	date
nengetsu	years and months
nenjū	whole year
nenkan	yearbook; almanac
nenkin	pension; annuity
nenmatsu	year-end
nen'nen	every year
nenrei	age; years
nenshi-mawari o suru	make a round of New Year's calls
neru	go to bed; sleep
nesage	reduction in price
nesshin(na)	enthusiastic
nesshin ni	enthusiastically
nesugosu	oversleep
netami	jealousy
netamu	be jealous
netsu	heat; fever
netsu ga aru	have a fever
nettō	boiling water
nezumi	mouse; rat
nī	two
ni	at; on; in; to; for
niau	suit; match well
nibai	twice
niban	second; number two
Nichi-Bei	Japan and America
nichiei-jiten	Japanese-English dictionary
nichiji	time and date

nichiyōbi	Sunday
nichiyōhin	daily necessities
nido	twice
nidome	second time
nieru	be cooked; be boiled
nigai	bitter
nigatsu	February
nigeru	flee; escape
nigiru	clutch; grasp; seize
nigiyaka(na)	animated; noisy
nihongo	Japanese language
nihonhū	Japanese style
nihonjin	Japanese person
nihonsei	made in Japan
niji	rainbow
nijisseiki	twentieth century
nijū	twenty
nikai	twice
nikibi	pimple
nikkei-beijin	Japanese-American
nikki	diary; journal
nikkō	sunshine; sunlight
nikoyaka(na)	smiling; beaming
niku	meat
nikuya	meat shop
nimotsu	baggage
ninen	two years
ningen	human being; man
ningensei	humanity
ningyō	doll; puppet
ninjin	carrot
ninki no aru	popular
ninshin suru	become pregnant
nioi	smell; odor
niou	(v.) smell
Nippon	Japan

niretsu	two rows
nishi	west
nishūkan	two weeks
nisoku	two pairs (of shoes, socks, etc.)
nisshabyō	sunstroke
nittei	day's schedule; itinerary
niwa	yard; garden
niwatori	chicken
nizukuri suru	pack up
no	of; at; in; on
nobasu	stretch; develop (one's talent)
nobasu	extend; postpone
nobiru	be extended; be postponed
noborizaka	uphill road
noboru	rise; go up
noboru	climb
nodo	throat
nodo ga itai	have a sore throat
nodo ga kawaku	feel thirsty
nodo ga tsumaru	be choked
nōgyō	agriculture; farming
nohara	field; plains
nōjō	farm
nokorimono	leftovers
nokoru	be left; remain
nokosu	leave behind; set aside
nomikomu	swallow; gulp
nomimizu	drinking water
nomimono	drink; beverage
nomisugiru	drink too much
nomu	(v.) drink
nonki(na)	easygoing; happy-go-lucky; carefree
nori	seaweed
nori	glue; paste; starch
norikaeru	change; transfer
norimaki	rolled <u>sushi</u>

noritsugu	make connection with (a bus)
noroi	slow; tardy
noseru	give a ride
nōson	farm village
nōzeisha	taxpayer
nozoku	peep; look in
nozomi	(n.) wish; hope
nozomu	(v.) wish; hope
nugu	take off; get undressed
nureru	get wet; be soaked
nureta	wet; moist; damp
nusumu	steal; rob
nuu	sew; stitch
nyūgaku-gansho	application form for admission
nyūgaku-shigansha	applicant for admission
nyūgaku-shiken	entrance examination
nyūgaku-shiken o ukeru	take an entrance examination
nyūgaku suru	be enrolled at a school
nyūjōken	admission ticket; platform ticket
nyūjōryō	admission fee
nyūkyosha	tenant
nyūsu	news

0.	o	tail
	ō	king; monarch
	oba	aunt
	ōbā	overcoat
	obāchan	grandma
	obasan	aunt; middle aged woman
	obāsan	grandmother; old woman
	oboeru	remember
	ōbosha	applicant
	ōbo suru	apply for
	ocha	tea
	ochiru	fall; drop
	ochitsuku	settle down; recover one's composure

ōdanhodō	pedestrian crossing; crosswalk
ōdan suru	cross; traverse
odori	(n.) dance
ōdōri	main street
odoroku	be surprised; be amazed
odoru	(v.) dance
ōen suru	give aid; support
ogawa	brook; stream
ōgoe de	in a loud voice; loudly
ogoru	give (a person) a treat
ōhuku-jōshaken	round-trip ticket
ōhuku suru	make a round trip
ōhuku-unchin	fare for a round trip
oi	nephew
ōi	plenty of
Oikoshi kinshi	No Passing.
oishii	tasty; delicious
oji	uncle
ojigi o suru	bow; make a bow
ojiisan	grandfather; old man
ojōsan	young woman; Miss
oka	hill
Okaeri nasai	Welcome home!; Welcome back!
okage de	thanks to (a person)
Okamainaku	Don't inconvenience yourself for my sake.
okane	money
okāsan	mother
okashii	funny; comical
okawari	another helping; another portion
ōkesutora	orchestra
ōkii	big; large; loud
okiru	get up; wake up
okòru	get angry
okōru	happen; occur; take place
oku	put; place
okugai(no)	outdoor; open-air; outside

okunai (no)	indoor
okuraseru	delay; put off
okureru	be late; be delayed
okurimono	present; gift
<u>okuru</u>	send; dispatch
<u>okuru</u>	give; confer
okusama	married woman; madam; your(his) wife
ōkyu-teate	first-aid treatment
omamori	good-luck charm
omatsuri	festival
Omedetō gozaimasu	Congratulations.
ōmisoka	New Year's Eve
omocha	toy
omoi	heavy; critical (condition)
omoidasu	recollect; recall
omoide	recollections; remembrances
omoiyari no aru	considerate; thoughtful
omo ni	mainly; chiefly
omosa	weight
omoshiroi	interesting; funny; enjoyable
omou	think; consider; believe; feel; hope
omuretsu	omelet
omutsu	diaper
onaji	same; equal
onaka	stomach
onaka ga suku	be hungry
onegai suru	ask; wish; request
ongaku	music
on'na	woman; female
on'na-no-ko	young girl; baby girl
onsen	hot spring
onshitsu	greenhouse
orenji-jūsu	orange juice
origami	paper-folding
orimono	textile; fabric
oriru	descend; get off

orosu	take down; bring down; let down; grate (cheese)
oru	break off; snap
ōsaji	tablespoon
Osaki e dozo	Please go ahead; After you.
osechi-ryōri	traditional Japanese dishes served on the first three days of the New Year
oseibo	year-end gift
osen suru	pollute; contaminate
ōsetsuma	drawing room
oshibori	hot towel; wet towel
oshidasu	push out
oshieru	teach; instruct; tell; coach
oshiire	closet; wall-cupboard
oshiri	backside; derriere
oshiroi	face powder
osoi	late; tardy; slow
osoku	late; slowly
osoku naru	be late; be behind time
osoroshii	fearful; dreadful
osou	attack
osowareru	be attacked
ossharu	say; speak; tell; talk
	* <u>ossharu</u> is the honorific form of the above English words.
osu	push
ōsugiru	too many; too much
otaku	your house
otearai	bathroom
otenki	weather
otenkiya	temperamental person
oto	sound; noise
ōtobai	motorcycle
otoko	man; male
otoko-no-ko	young boy; baby boy
otona	adult
otonashii	gentle; quiet

otōsan	father
otoshidama	money given as a gift at the New Year
otoshimono	lost article
otosu	drop; let fall
otōto	younger brother
ototoi	day before yesterday
ototoshi	year before last
otozureru	visit; call on
otsuri	(n.) change
otto	husband
ou	chase; pursue
ōuridashi	special bargain sale
owari	(n.) end; close; finish
owari made	to the end; till the last
owaru	end; close; complete
oya	parent
ōya	landlord; house-renter
oyako-kankei	parent-child relationship
oyakusho-shigoto	bureaucracy; red tape
oyogu	swim; have a swim
oyoso	about; nearly
ōzei (no)	many

P.	pachinko	pinball game
	pāma	perm; permanent
	pan	bread; roll; bun
	panhuretto	pamphlet; brochure
	panku suru	have a flat tire
	pantī	panties
	pantī-sutokkingu	panty hose
	pantsu	underpants; briefs; shorts
	panya	bakery; baker
	pāsento	percent
	pasokon	personal computer
	pasupōto	passport
	pātī	party

patokā	patrol car
pāto-taimā	part-time worker
pēji	page
pianisuto	pianist
piano o hiku	play the piano
pīman	green pepper
pinpon	ping-pong; table tennis
piza	pizza
pokapoka suru	feel comfortably warm
poketto	pocket
pondo	pound
posuto	mailbox
potapota ochiru	drip; fall in drops
purasuchikku	plastic
purattohōmu	railroad station platform
purezento	present
puroguramu	program
puro-yakyū	professional baseball
pūru	swimming pool
pyonpyon tobu	hop; skip

R.	raigetsu	next month
	raishun	next spring
	rainen	next year
	rainichi suru	come to Japan
	raishū	next week
	rajio	radio
	rakkanteki (na)	optimistic
	rakkasei	peanut
	raku (na)	comfortable
	rakudaiten	failing mark
	rakugaki	graffiti
	rakutenka	optimist
	rakutenteki (na)	optimistic
	rāmen	Chinese noodles
	ranchi	lunch

rasshu-awā ni	at rush hours
rei	bow
rei	example
rei	zero
reibō-sōchi	air conditioner; air conditioning
reibō suru	air-condition
reigai	exception
reigisahō	courtesy; etiquette
reijō	thank-you letter
reika	below zero
reiten	no marks; zero
reitō-shokuhin	frozen food
reizōko	refrigerator
rekishi	history
rekishiteki (na)	historical; traditional
rekōdo	record; disc
remon	lemon
ren'ai suru	fall in love
renkyū	consecutive holidays
renraku suru	contact; notify
renshū	practice; training; drill; exercise
renta-kā	rental car; Rent-a-Car
resutoran	restaurant
retsu	row; line
retsu ni narabu	line up; stand in a line
rieki	profit
rihatsuten	barber shop
rika	science
rikai suru	understand
rikishi	<u>sumo</u> wrestler
rikkyō	foot-bridge
rikon	(n.) divorce
rikō (na)	bright; smart; intelligent
rikoteki (na)	selfish; self-centered
ringo	apple
rinyūshoku	baby food

rippa(na)	great; superb
rirekisho	curriculum vitae; resume
risshoku	buffet
risu	squirrel
riyō suru	take advantage of; avail oneself
riyū	reason; cause
rōdō	labor
rōdō-jikan	working hours
rōka	corridor; hallway
rokubai	six times
rokuga suru	(v.) videotape
rokugatsu	June
rokujū	sixty
ronbun	essay; thesis; article
rōnin	high-school graduate who failed to enter a college waiting for another chance to be accepted
rōsoku	candle
rōsuto-bēhu	roast beef
rotenburo	open-air bath
rotō ni mayou	become homeless
ruigo	synonym
rusu	being away from home
ryō	fishing
ryō	dormitory
ryōgae	money exchange
ryōgawa	both sides
ryohi	traveling expenses
ryōhō	both
ryōjikan	consulate
ryokan	Japanese hotel
ryoken	passport
ryōkin	charge; fee
ryōkinjo	tollbooth
ryokō	journey; travel; trip; tour
ryokō-gaisha	travel agency
ryokō-nittei	itinerary; travel schedule

ryokōsha	traveler; tourist
ryokō suru	travel; make a trip
ryokucha	green tea
ryōmen	both sides
ryōri	cooking; dish
ryōrinin	cook
ryōshin	parents
ryōshūsho	receipt
ryūchō(na)	fluent
ryūgakusei	foreign student
ryūgaku suru	study abroad
ryūkō(no)	fashionable; in fashion
sa	difference
sabishii	lonely; lonesome
sābisuryō	service charge
saboru	cut (a class)
sadō	tea ceremony
sagasu	look for; search
sahō	manners; etiquette
saigai	disaster
saigo ni	in conclusion; eventually
saigo made	to the end
saihakkō suru	reissue
saihu	purse; wallet; pocketbook
saijitsu	national holiday
saikakunin	reconfirmation
saikin	recently; lately
saikō(no)	highest; maximum; best
Saimatsu ōuridashi	Year-end Sale.
sain	sign; signature; autograph
saishiken	reexamination; makeup exam
saisho kara	from the beginning
saisho ni	first; in the first place
saiteki(na)	optimum
saiten suru	(v.) grade; mark; score

saiwai	happiness; good luck
saizen o tsukusu	do one's best
saizu	size
saka	slope; hill
sakaeru	prosper
sakana	fish
sake	sake; liquor
sake	salmon
sakebu	shout; scream
sakeru	avoid; avert
sakka	writer; novelist
sakki	some time ago; a little while ago
sakkyū ni	urgently
saku	fence; railing
saku	bloom; blossom
sakuban	last night
sakubun	essay; composition
sakuhin	work; production
sakujitsu	yesterday
sakura	cherry tree; cherry blossoms
sakuranbo	cherry
sakusen	tactics; strategy
sakusha	author; writer
sakuya	last night; yesterday evening
samo-nakereba	otherwise; if not so
samui	cold; chilly
samuke ga suru	feel a chill
san	three
san	Mr.; Mrs.; Miss
sanbai	three times
sanbashi	pier; wharf
sando	three times
sandoicchi	sandwiches
sangatsu	March
sangurasu	sunglasses
sangyō	industry

sanhujinka	obstetrics and gynecology
sanjū	thirty
sanka suru	participate; take part in
sankasha	participant
sankōsho	reference book
san'nen	three years
san'nin	three people
sanpatsu suru	have a haircut
sanpo suru	take a walk
sanrui	third base
sansai	three years old
sansei suru	agree; approve
sanshin	strikeout
sansū	arithmetic
Santa Kurōsu	Santa Claus
sara	plate; dish; saucer
sarada	salad
saraigetsu	month after next
sara ni	furthermore; moreover
srarīman	salaried man; white-collar worker
saru	monkey
saru	leave; depart
sasayaku	(v.) whisper; murmur
sashiageru	give; present
	* sashiageru is the honorific expression of give and present.
sashidashi-nin	sender; addresser
sashimi	slices of raw fish
sashō	visa
sassoku	at once; immediately
sasu	point to; indicate; name
satō	sugar
satsumaimo	sweet potato
sawagashii	noisy; boisterous
sawagu	make a fuss
sawaru	(v.) touch

sayōnara	good-bye
se	(n.) back
sei	family name
seibetsu	gender
seihuku	uniform
seihin	product; goods
seiji	politics
seijika	statesman; politician
seijin	adult
seijiteki (na)	political
seijitsu (na)	sincere; faithful
seikaku ni	accurately; precisely
seikaku	character; personality
seikatsu	life; livelihood
seikatsuhi	living expenses; cost of living
seikatsu-yōshiki	life-style; way of life
seiketsu (na)	clean; neat
seiki	century
seikō suru	succeed; be successful
sei-kyōiku	sex education
sēimei	life
sēimei	one's full name
seimei-hoken	life insurance
seinen	youth; young man
seinen-gappi	date of birth
seisan suru	produce; manufacture
seisanteki (na)	productive
seisekihyō	report card
seishin	mind; soul; spirit
seishin-hakujakusha	the mentally handicapped
seishinkai	psychiatrist
seishinteki (na)	mental; spiritual
seishitsu	nature; disposition; character
seito	pupil; student
seiyōka	Westernization
sekai	world

seki	(n.) cough
sekidome	cough medicine
sekihan	festive red rice
sekinin	responsibility
sekinin ga aru	be responsible for
seki ni tsuku	take one's seat
sekken	soap
semai	narrow; small
sen	one thousand
sen	line
sen	stopper; cork
senaka	one's back
senbetsu	farewell gift
senden	publicity
senden suru	advertise; propagandize
sengetsu	last month
senjitsu	the other day; some time ago
senkō-bunya	field of specialization
senkō suru	specialize in; major in
senmenjo	washroom
senmon	speciality; special subject
senmonka	specialist
sen'nen suru	devote oneself to
sen'nuki	corkscrew; bottle opener
senpai	one's senior
sensei	teacher; master; doctor
senshu	player; athlete
senshū	last week
sensō	war
sensu	folding fan
sentaku	washing; laundry
sentaku-kamoku	elective subject
sentakuki	washing machine
sentaku ni dasu	take (it) to a cleaner's
sentaku suru	wash; do the laundry
sentakuya	cleaner's

sentō	public bath
senyaku ga aru	have a previous appointment
senzai	detergent
seruhu-sābisu	self-service
sērusuman	traveling salesman
sētā	sweater
setomono	china; porcelain
setsumei	explanation
setsumei suru	explain
setsuyaku suru	economize; save
settoku suru	persuade
sewa o suru	take care of; look after
shakai	society; world
shakai-hukushi	social welfare
shakaika	social studies
shakai-mondai	social problem
shakkuri	hiccough
shako	garage
shakōteki(na)	sociable
shanai	inside a car(train, bus, etc.)
shasen	traffic lane
shashin	photograph
shashin o toru	take a picture of
shawā o abiru	take a shower
shī	city
shī	four
shi	poetry
shī	death
shī	hush!; sshh!
shiageru	finish; complete
shiai	match; game
shiawase(na)	happy; fortunate
shiba	grass; lawn
shibaraku	for a while
shibashiba	often; frequently
shibushibu	reluctantly; half-heartedly

shichi	seven
shichigatsu	July
shichi-go-san	gala day for children of three, five and seven years of age
shichimenchō	turkey
shichiya	pawnshop
shichō	mayor
shidō suru	direct; coach; instruct; guide
shidōsha	director; instructor; leader; coarch
shigai-kyokuban	area code
shigansha	applicant; candidate; volunteer
shigatsu	April
shigen	resources
shigoto	work; job; business
shigoto ga aru	have work to do; have business to attend to
shigoto ga nai	be out of work; be jobless
shigyōshiki	opening ceremony of the school year; convocation
shihainin	manager (at a hotel, a restaurant, etc.)
shiharai	payment
shiharau	pay
shijin	poet
shijō	market
shika	deer
shikaisha	MC; chairperson; toastmaster
shikata ga nai	cannot help (it); (it) cannot be helped
shiken	examination; test
shiken o ukeru	take an examination
shikenteki (na)	experimental; tentative
shikī	four seasons
shikī	ceremony; rituals
shikin o atsumeru	raise funds; collect funds
Shikkari shinasai	Cheer up!; Take courage!
shikke	humidity; moisture
shikke no ōoi	humid; moist; damp
shikyū	urgently; at once

shima	island
shimaru	be closed; shut
shimei	full name
shimekiri-kijitsu	deadline
shimeppoi	damp; wet
shimeru	tie; tighten
shimesu	show; point; indicate
shimi	stain; spot
shimin	citizen
shiminken	citizenship
shimo	frost
shimon	fingerprints
Shinagire	Out of stock
shinamono	article; goods
shin-Bei	pro-American
shinbō suru	be patient; endure
shinbōzuyoi	patient; persevering
shinbun	newspaper
shinbunsha	newspaper company
shindaisha	sleeping car; sleeper
shindan suru	diagnose
shingakki	new school term
shingaku	theology
shingō	signal; traffic light
shinjiru	believe; trust; have faith
shinjitsu	truth; fact; reality
shinju	pearl
shinkansen	<u>Shinkansen</u>; bullet train
shinkon-ryokō	(n.) honeymoon
shinku-sōjiki	vacuum cleaner
shinmitsu(na)	intimate; close
<u>shin</u>´nen	belief; conviction
<u>shin</u>´nen	the New Year
Shin´nen omedetō	Happy New Year!
shin-Nichika	Japanophile
shinpai(na)	anxious; worried

shinpaigoto	worries; troubles
shinpai suru	worry; care; be troubled
shinpiteki(na)	mysterious
shinpo	progress; advance
shinpoteki(na)	advanced; progressive
shinri	truth
shinrigaku	psychology
shinrō-shinpu	bride and bridegroom
shinrui	relatives
shinryōjo	clinic; medical office
shinsatsu o ukeru	see a doctor; consult a physician
shinsen(na)	fresh; new
shinsetsu(na)	kind; hospitable
shinsetsu ni	kindly
shinshitsu	bedroom
shintai-shōgaisha	physically handicapped person
Shinto	Shintoism; <u>Shinto</u>
shinu	die
shin'yū	one's best friend; close friend
shio	salt
shippai suru	fail; make a mistake
shiraberu	examine; investigate
shiriai	acquaintance
shiro	(n.) white
shiro	castle
shiroi	(adj.) white
shiru	know
shiseki	historic site
shisho	librarian
shishobako	post-office box
shishunki	adolescence
shita	tongue
shitagau	obey; follow
shitagi	underwear
shitashii	intimate; friendly
shitei-seki	reserved seat

shiteki (na)	private; personal
shitsubō suru	be disappointed
shitsudo	humidity
shitsugyō suru	lose one's job
shitsumon	question; inquiry
shitsumon suru	ask a question; interrogate
shitsurei (na)	impolite; rude; discourteous
Shitsurei shimasu	Excuse me.
shitto	jealousy
shitto suru	be jealous
Shiyōchū	Occupied.
shizen	nature
shizen (na)	natural; unartificial
shizen ni	naturally; automatically
shizuka (na)	quiet; silent
Shizuka ni	Keep still.
shizumu	sink; go down
shō	prize
shōdaku	consent; agreement
shodana	bookshelf
shōgakkō	elementary school
shōgakukin	scholarship; student loan
shōgakusei	school children
shōgatsu	the New Year's Day
shōgo	noon; noontime
shohōsen	prescription
shōji	shoji screen
shōjiki (na)	honest
shōjo	little girl; young girl
shōka	digestion
shōka-huryō	indigestion
shōkai	introduction
shōkaijō	letter of introduction
shōkai suru	introduce
shokki	tableware
shōko	evidence; proof

shokubutsu	plant; flora
shokudō	dining room
shokudōsha	dining car
shokugyō	occupation; profession; job
shokuin	staff member; personnel
shokuji	meal
shokumotsu	food
shokuryō	food; provisions
shokutaku	table
shokutsū	gourmet
shokuyoku	appetite for food
shokuyoku ga nai	have no appetite
shokyū	beginner's class
shomei suru	sign one's name
shōmeisho	certificate
shōnika	pediatrics
shorai	future
shorui	document; papers
shosai	study; den
shōsetsu	novel; fiction
shoshinsha	beginner
shōtai suru	invite
shōtaijō	letter of invitation
shoten	bookstore
shōten	store; shop
shōten	focus
shotoku	income
shōyu	soy sauce
shoyūsha	owner
shū	state, e. g., New York
shū	week
shucchō suru	make a business trip; take an official trip
shuchō suru	insist; assert; claim
shudai	subject; theme
shudōken	leadership
shūgaku-ryokō	school excursion

shuhu	housewife
shūji	calligraphy
shūjitsu	weekday
shūkan	custom; habit
shukudai	assignment; homework
shukuen	banquet; feast
shukuhaku suru	lodge in; check in
shukuhuku	blessing
shukujitsu	national holiday
shukyō	religion
shūmatsu	weekend
shumi	hobby; interest
shunyū	income; earnings
shuppan suru	publish; issue
shuppatsu	departure
shuppatsu suru	depart; leave
shūri suru	repair; mend; fix
shurui	kind; sort; variety
shushō	prime minister
shūshoku suru	find work; get a position
shussan suru	give birth
shusseki	attendance; presence
shūten	terminal station; last stop
shūtome	mother-in-law
shuwa	sign language
shūyō	accommodation; seating
sō desu	I hear; they say; it is said
soba	buckwheat noodles
sōbetsukai	farewell party
sobo	grandmother
sochira	there; over there; that one
sōdan suru	consult
sodateru	bring up; raise
sodatsu	grow up; be brought up
sode	sleeve
sōgo(no)	mutual; reciprocal

sohu	grandfather
sohubo	grandparents
sōji	cleaning
sōkō-kyori	mileage
sokudo	speed; pace
sokudo o otosu	slow down
sokudo-seigen	speed limit
sokutatsu	special delivery
sōmei (na)	wise; bright
songai	damage
sonkei suru	(v.) respect; esteem; honor
Son'nahazu wa nai	That can't be.
sonoaida	during the time
sonogo	after that; from that time on
sonotame	for that reason
Sono tōri	That's right.
sora	sky
sore	that; it
sorekara	after that; and then
soremade	till then
sōridaijin	prime minister
soroban	abacus
sorosoro	slowly; gradually
soru	shave
sōseiji	twin
sōsēji	sausage
sōsobo	great-grandmother
sōsohu	great-grandfather
soto	outside
sotsugyōsei	(n.) graduate
sotsugyō-shiki	commencement; graduation ceremony
sotsugyō-shōsho	diploma
sotsugyō suru	graduate from
sōzō suru	imagine
sōzōteki (na)	creative
su	vinegar

suashi	bare feet
subarashii	splendid; excellent; wonderful
suberu	slide; slip
subete	all; everything; entirely
sude ni	already
sūgaku	mathematics
sugata	figure; shape
sugoi	superb
sugu	at once; right away
suiei	swimming
suika	watermelon
suimin	(n.) sleep
suisenjō	letter of recommendation
suisen suru	recommend
suiyōbi	Wednesday
suji	figure; numeral
sujigaki	(n.) outline; plot
sūkagetsu	several months
sūkai	several times
sukāto	skirt
suki de aru	like; care for; love
sukī	skiing
suki-kirai	likes and dislikes
sukizuki	matter of taste
sukoshi	a little; a few; a little while
sukuu	rescue; save; help
sumi	corner; nook
sumō	<u>sumo</u> wrestling
sumu	live; reside
suna	sand
sunawachi	namely; that is to say
sūpā-māketto	supermarket
supīdo o otosu	reduce speed
supōtsu o suru	play sports
suri	pickpocket
suru	do (something); make (a decision, an excuse, etc.);

	have (a walk, a talk, etc.)
sushizume(no)	jam-packed
susugu	rinse
suteki(na)	lovely; cute
suteru	throw away
suwaru	take a seat; sit down
suzushii	cool; refreshing
tabako	tobacco
tabako o suu	(v.) smoke
tabemono	food
tabe-nokoshi	leftover food
taberu	eat
tabesugi	overeating
tabi	traveling; journey; tour
tabitabi	often
tabun	perhaps
Tachiiri kinshi	Keep off!
tachiyoru	stop at; drop in on
tada de	for free; without charge
Tadaima	Hello. I'm back.
tadashii	right; correct
taido	attitude
taigaku suru	drop out of school (college)
Tiheiyō	Pacific Ocean
taihen(na)	serious; awful
taiiku	physical education
taiin suru	leave hospital
taiken suru	(v.) experience
taiko	drum
taikutsu(na)	boring
taikutsu suru	be bored
taion o hakaru	take one's temperature
tairiku	continent
Taiseiyō	Atlantic Ocean
taisetsu(na)	important
taisetsu ni suru	cherish; treasure

taishi	ambassador
taishikan	embassy
taisō	gymnastics
taitei	mostly; largely
taiyō	sun
taizai suru	stay over; sojourn
takai	high; tall; expensive
takara	treasure
takarakuji	public lottery
take	bamboo
taki	waterfall; cascade
takusan(no)	much; great deal of; many
takushī	taxi
tamago	egg
tama ni	occasionally; once in a while
tamaranai	cannot refrain from
tamashii	soul
tameiki	(n.) sigh
tame ni	for the sake of; in favor of; in order to; on account of
tameru	save; store
tamesu	(v.) try; attempt
tana	shelf
tanbo	rice field
tango	word
Tango no sekku	Boy's Festival
tani	valley
tanjōbi	birthday
tanjō suru	be born
tanken	exploration; expedition
tanki-daigaku	junior college
tan'nō(na)	proficient; skillful
tanomu	ask; beg; request
tanoshii	merry; joyous
tanoshiku	merrily; joyfully
tanoshimu	enjoy; have a good time

tantōsha	person in charge
taoreru	fall; fall over
taosu	bring down; fell; get (a person) down; defeat
tarinai	be not enough; be short of
tariru	be sufficient; be adequate
tashika(na)	sure; certain
tashika ni	certainly; definitely
tasu	add; supply
tasukaru	be saved
tasuke	(n.) help; aid; support
tasukeru	help; save; rescue
tatakau	go to war; fight
tataku	strike; beat; hit
tatamu	fold; fold up
tatemono	building
tatoeba	for instance; for example
tatsu	stand up; stand
tayori	news; tidings
tayoru	rely on; count on
tazuneru	visit; call on
tazuneru	seek; ask; inquire
te	hand; arm; paw
tebiki	guidance; manual; guidebook
tebukuro	gloves; mittens
tēburu	table
tegami	letter
teian	proposition; proposal
teian suru	propose; suggest
teika	labeled price
teikiken	pass; commuter's ticket
teinei(na)	polite; courteous; thorough
teisha suru	stop (at a station)
tekiōsei	adaptability; flexibility
tekiō suru	be adapted to; adjust oneself to
tekisetsu(na)	appropriate; adequate
tekitō(na)	proper; suitable

tekitō ni	adequately; properly
tekubi	wrist
ten	sky; heaven
ten	spot; dot; point; grades; score
te ni amaru	be beyond one's control
tenimotsu	luggage; baggage
tenimotsu-ichiji-azukarijo	checkroom
ten'in	salesclerk
tenji	exhibition; display
tenji	Braille
tenjō	ceiling
tenki	weather
tenkiyohō	weather forecast
tenkō	weather
ten'nō	emperor
tenpura	deep-fried fish or vegetable
tenrankai	exhibition; show
tenshoku	vocation
tensō suru	transmit; forward
tensū	marks; score
tenugui	hand towel
tera	temple
terebi	TV
tetsudai	help; assistant
tetsudau	help; assist
tetsudō	railroad; railway
tetsugaku	philosophy
tezukuri (no)	handmade; homemade
to	door
tō	ten
tō	tower; pagoda
tōan	examination paper
tobira	door
tobu	jump; leap; hop
tōchaku	arrival
tōchaku suru	arrive; reach

tochū de	on one's way
tōdai	lighthouse
todana	cupboard; cabinet
todokeru	send; deliver
tohyō suru	vote; cast a ballot
tōi	far; distant
toiawase	inquiry; reference
toi-awaseru	inquire; make inquiries
toire	bathroom; restroom
tojiru	close; shut
tōka	for ten days; the tenth of a month
tokai	city
tokei	clock; watch
tokeru	melt
toki	time; hour; occasion
tōki	chinaware; ceramics
tokidoki	sometimes
tokkyū	super-express
toko-no-ma	alcove
tokoro	place
tokoro de	by the way
tokoya	barber
tōku kara	from afar
tokubetsu(no)	special
tokubetsu ni	especially
tomaru	(v.) stop; halt
tomaru	lodge; stay; check in
tomeru	stop; fasten
tomodachi	friend; companion
tomodachi ni naru	make friends with
tōmorokoshi	corn
tōnan ni au	be robbed; be stolen
tonari(no)	next; neighboring
tonkatsu	pork cutlet
toraberāzu-chekku	traveler's check
toranpu o suru	play cards

tori	bird; chicken
torihiki	transactions; dealings
torikaeru	exchange; change
toriniku	chicken
tōroku suru	register; enroll
toru	take; seize
tōru	pass; walk over; get through
tōsen suru	be elected
toshī	year; age
tōshi	city
toshiyori	old people
toshokan	library
tōshu	pitcher
tōsuto	(n.) toast
totemo	(cannot) possibly; very
tōza-yokin	checking account
tozan	mountain-climbing
tsubasa	wings
tsubusu	crush; smash
tsuchi	soil; earth
tsue	walking stick; cane
tsugi(no)	next; following
tsugitsugi ni	one by one; one after another
tsugō no ii	convenient; suitable
tsui ni	at last; finally
tsuiseki	pursuit; chase
tsui-shiken	makeup examination
tsui-shiken o ukeru	take a makeup exam
tsuitachi	the first day of a month
tsukai	errand
tsukamaeru	catch; seize
tsukamu	seize; hold; grasp
tsukare	fatigue; exhaustion
tsukareru	get tired; become exhausted
tsukau	use; manipulate; spend
tsukemono	pickles

tsuki	moon; month
tsukiau	associate with; keep company with
tsuki-hajime	beginning of the month
tsukihi	months and days
tsūkin suru	commute
tsūkonin	passerby; pedestrian
Tsūkodome	Road closed; Closed to traffic.
tsuku	adhere to; reach; arrive at
tsuku	thrust; pierce
tsukue	desk
tsukuri-kata	how to make
tsukuru	make; create; manufacture
tsuma	wife
tsumaranai	boring; trivial
tsumazuku	stumble; trip over
tsume	nail; claw; hoof
tsumetai	cold
tsurara	icicle
tsurete-iku	take (a person, an animal)
tsurete-kuru	bring (a person, an animal)
tsuri	fishing; change
tsūro	passageway; aisle
tsuru	crane
tsuru	have a cramp
tsutomeru	serve (in a company); fill (a post)
tsutsumi-gami	wrapping paper
tsutsumu	wrap; pack
tsūyaku	interpretation; interpreter
tsuyoi	strong; powerful; healthy
tsuyu	rainy season
tsuyu	dew; dewdrop
tsuzukeru	continue
tsuzuku	continue; last
tsuzuri	spelling; orthography
tsuzuru	spell

U.	uchi	house
	uchijū	whole family
	uchiwa	round paper fan
	ude	arm
	udedokei	wristwatch
	udon	noodles
	ue	on; over; above; up; upstairs; top
	ueki	garden tree; potted plant
	ueru	(v.) plant
	ueru	starve
	ue-shita	up and down; above and below
	uesuto	waist
	uetoresu	waitress
	ugokasu	move; operate
	ugoki	movement; motion
	ugoku	move; work
	uisuki	whisky
	ukagau	visit; call on; inquire; hear
		* ukagau is the humble expression of visit and listen.
	ukeireru	accept
	ukeru	catch; receive; take (an examination)
	uketoru	receive
	uketsuke	receptionist; reception desk
	ukkari	absentmindedly
	uma	horse
	umai	tasty; good
	umaku	well; skillfully
	umareru	be born
	ume	Japanese plum
	umeboshi	pickled Japanese plum
	umi	sea; ocean
	umu	bear; give birth to
	undō	exercise; sport
	undōkai	athletic meet
	un ga ii	be fortunate

un o tamesu	take a chance
unten suru	drive
unzari suru	be disgusted with
uo	fish
uo-ichiba	fish market
uraguchi	back door
uranai	fortune-telling
urayamu	envy; be envious
ureru	ripen
ureshii	glad; happy
uriage	sales
uridashi	bargain sale; clearance sale
urikireru	be sold out
uru	sell
urusai	noisy; annoying; be fastidious
ushi	cattle; cow; bull; ox
ushinau	lose; miss; be deprived of
ushiro	(n.) back; rear; behind
uso	lie; fib
uso o tsuku	tell a lie
usui	thin; weak (tea, coffee); light (c
uta	song; poem
utagau	doubt; suspect
utagawashii	doubtful; unreliable; suspicious
utau	sing; chant; carol
utsu	strike; hit
utsukushii	beautiful; pretty
utsusu	reflect; mirror
utsusu	take a picture of; copy
uwagi	coat; jacket
uwasa	rumor; gossip
wabiru	apologize
wadai	topic
waei-jiten	Japanese-English dictionary
wagamama(na)	selfish; self-centered

wahū	Japanese style
wahuku	traditional Japanese costume; kimono
waishatsu	shirt
wakai	young; junior
wakame	seaweed
wakamono	the young
wakareru	part; separate
wakari-nikui	difficult to understand
Wakari mashita	I see; I understand.
wakari-yasui	easy to understand
wakaru	understand; know
wakasu	boil (water)
wakimichi	side road
waki-no-shita	armpit
wakuwaku suru	be excited over
wameku	(v.) shout
wan	bay; gulf
warau	laugh; smile
wareyasui	breakable
waribashi	disposable wooden chopsticks
waribiki	(n.) discount
waribiki suru	(v.) discount
warikan ni suru	go Dutch treat
warizan	division
waru	divide
warui	bad; wrong
warukuchi o iu	speak ill of; speak against
wasabi	Japanese horseradish
washitsu	Japanese-style room
washoku	Japanese-style meal
wasuremono	article left behind
wasureppoi	forgetful
wasureru	forget; leave behind
wataru	go across; go over
watashi	I
watashi no	my

watashi o	me
watashitachi	we
watashitachi no	our
watashitachi o	us
watasu	give; hand over
wayō-secchū	blending of Japanese and Western styles
waza to	on purpose; intentionally
wazurawasu	bother

Y.

yachin	(n.) rent
yado	inn; hotel
yakamashii	noisy
yakan	kettle
yakedo	(n.) burn; scald
yakedo o suru	get scorched; get scalded
yakeru	be burned; be sunburned; be baked
yakimono	pottery; porcelain
yakitori	chicken shish kebab
yakkyoku	drugstore; pharmacy
yaku	translation
yakudatsu	be useful; be helpful
yakusho	government office
yakusoku	(n.) promise
yakusoku suru	(v.) promise
yakusu	translate; interpret
yakuza	gangster
yakyū	baseball
yama	mountain; hill
yameru	stop; cease
yamū	stop; cease; drop; end
yamu o enai	beyond one's control
yane	roof
yanushi	house owner
yaoya	vegetable store
yarikata	way; method; process
yarinaosu	do over again

yarinikui	difficult to do
yaru	give; present; do
yasai	vegetables
yasashii	gentle; tender
yasashii	easy; simple
yaseru	lose weight
yasui	cheap; inexpensive
yasumi	rest; break; intermission; holiday; absence
yasumu	take a rest; be absent; skip (school); go to bed
yasuuri	bargain sale
yatou	employ
yatowareru	be employed
yatto	at last; with much effort
yawarakai	soft; tender
yayakoshii	complicated
yōbi	day of the week
yobikō	cram school
yobirin	doorbell
yobō suru	prevent; protect from
yobu	call; invite
yōchien	kindergarten; preschool
yōchi(na)	childish; immature
yō ga aru	have something to do; have business with
yogoreru	become dirty
yogoreta	dirty
yogosu	make (a thing) dirty; stain
yōgu	tool; instrument; appliance
yohō	(n.) forecast
yōhuku	Western clothes
yoi	good; fine
yōi	preparation; arrangements
yōi ga dekiteiru	be ready for
yōi suru	prepare for; get ready for
yōji	baby; preschool child
yōji	toothpick
yōji ga aru	have something to do

yōjin suru	be cautious of
yōka	eight days; the eighth day of a month
yōkan	sweet red-bean jelly
yokin	bank account; savings
yōki (na)	cheerful; merry
yoki suru	enticipate
yokka	four days; the fourth day of a month
yoku	well; nicely; thoroughly
yōkyū suru	require; demand; request
yomeru	be able to read; be readable
yomi-kaki	reading and writing
yominikui	hard to read
yomiyasui	easy to read
yomu	read
yonaka	midnight
yonen	four years
yonensei	fourth-year pupil; senior
yonjū	forty
yopparai	drunk; drunken person
yopparau	get drunk
yori	than
yorisou	get close; snuggle against
yorokobu	be glad; rejoice
yoron	public opinion
yoroshii	fine; good; all right
yoroshiiyō ni	as you like it
yoru	night
yosan	budget
yōshi	adopted son
yoshū	preparation of a lesson
yoshū suru	prepare lessons
yosōdōri	as was expected
yosō suru	anticipate
yotei	(n.) plan; schedule
yottsu	four
you	get drunk

yowai	weak; frail
yoyaku	reservation
yoyaku suru	make a reservation
yu	hot water; hot bath
yūbe	last night
yūben(na)	eloquent; fluent
yubi	finger; toe
yūbin	mail; mail service
yūbin-bangō	zip code
yūbin-hagaki	postal card
yūbin-haitatsu	mailman
yūbin-kitte	postage stamp
yūbinkyoku	post office
yūbin-ryōkin	postage
yūbin´uke	mailbox
yubisasu	point at
yubiwa	ring
yūbō(na)	promising; hopeful
yūdachi	shower
yūeki(na)	beneficial; useful
yūenchi	amusement park
yūgata	early evening
yūhan	supper; dinner
yūhi	setting sun
yūhuku(na)	wealthy; affluent
yūjō	friendship
yuka	floor
yūkan	evening paper
yūkan(na)	brave; courageous
yukata	informal summer kimono
yuki	snow
yukidaruma	snowman
yūki o dasu	gather one´s courage
yukkuri	slowly; leisurely
yume	(n.) dream
yume o miru	(v.) dream

yūmei (na)	famous; well-known
yūmoa	humor
yunyū suru	(v.) import
yu o wakasu	boil water
yūransen	sightseeing boat
yurusu	permit; allow
yūshoku	supper; dinner
yushutsu suru	(v.) export
yutaka (na)	wealthy; abundant
yūtosei	honor student
zabuton	floor cushion
zaiseiteki-enjo	financial support
zaitaku suru	be at home
zangyō	overtime work
zan´nen (na)	regrettable
zan´nen nagara	regrettably; unfortunately
zaseki	seat
zaseki-bangō	seat number
zashiki	tatami-matted room
zasshi	magazine; periodical
zatsudan suru	have a chat
zatsuyō	chores
zehi	by all means; at any cost
zeikan	customs
zeikin	tax
zeitaku (na)	luxurious; extravagant
zekkō suru	break up with
zenbu	all
zengo	before and after
zen´in	all the members
zenjitsu	previous day
zenki	first term; first semester
zenkoku	whole country
zenryoku o tsukusu	do one's best
zensekai	whole world

zenshin suru	(v.) advance
zen-sokuryoku de	at full speed
zentai(no)	whole; entire
zenzen	(not) at all
zerī	jello
zessan suru	admire
zetsubō suru	despair
zetsubōteki(na)	desperate
zettai ni	absolutely; by no means
zō	elephant
zō	image; statue
zōge	ivory
zōka	artificial flower
zōka suru	increase
zokugo	(n.) slang
zoku suru	belong to; be affiliated with
zokuzoku	one after another; successively
zōni	soup with rice cakes and vegetables
zonzai(na)	rude; careless
zōri	Japanese sandals
zu	illustration; chart
zubon	trousers
zuhyō	chart; diagram
zuibun	very
zukan	illustrated book
zuruyasumi o suru	play hooky
zutsū	headache
zutsū ga suru	have a headache

HIPPOCRENE EAST ASIAN TITLES

Cambodian-English/English-Cambodian
Standard Dictionary
**15,000 entries • 355 pages • 5½ x 8¼ •
ISBN 0-87052-818-1 • $16.95pb • (143)**

Cantonese Basic Course
**416 pages • 5½ x 8½ • ISBN 0-7818-0289-X • $19.95pb
• (117)**

Dictionary of 1,000 Chinese Proverbs
**200 pages • 5 ½ x 8 ½ • ISBN 0-7818-0682-8 • $11.95pb
• (773)**

Dictionary of 1,000 Chinese Idioms
**167 pages • 6 x 9 • ISBN 0-7818-0820-0 •
$14.95pb • (598)**

Chinese Handy Dictionary
**2,000 entries • 120 pages • 5 x 7 ¾ •
ISBN 0-87052-050-4 • $8.95pb • (347)**

English-Chinese Pinyin Dictionary
**10,000 entries • 500 pages • 4 x 6 •
ISBN 0-7818-0427-2 • $19.95pb • (509)**

Chinese-English Dictionary of the
500 Most Used Words
A Study Guide to Mandarin Chinese
**500 entries • 200 pages • 5½ x 8½ •
ISBN 0-7818-0842-1 • $16.95pb • (277)**

Hippocrene Children's Illustrated Chinese
Dictionary (Mandarin)
500 entries • 94 pages • 8½ x 11
paperback: **ISBN 0-7818-0848-0 • $11.95 • (662)**
hardcover: **ISBN 0-7818-0834-0 • $14.95 • (174)**

Beginner's Chinese
**150 pages • 5½ x 8 • ISBN 0-7818-0566-X •
$14.95pb • (690)**

English-Ilocano Dictionary and Phrasebook
**7,000 entries • 269 pages • 5½ x 8½ •
ISBN 0-7818-0642-9 • $14.95pb • (718)**

Indonesian-English/English-Indonesian
Practical Dictionary
**17,000 entries • 289 pages • 4¼ x 7 •
ISBN 0-87052-810-6 • $11.95pb • (127)**

Speak Standard Indonesian
**285 pages • 4 x 6 • ISBN 0-7818-0186-9 • $11.95pb •
(115)**

Japanese Handy Dictionary
3,400 entries • 120 pages • 5 x 7 •
ISBN 0-87052-962-5 • $8.95pb • (466)

Japanese-English/English-Japanese
Dictionary and Phrasebook
2,300 entries • 220 pages • 3¾ x 7 •
ISBN 0-7818-0814-6 • $12.95pb • (205)

Beginner's Japanese
200 pages • 5 x 8 • ISBN 0-7818-0234-2 •
$11.95pb • (53)

Mastering Japanese
368 pages • 5½ x 8½ • ISBN 0-87052-983 • $14.95pb •
(523)
2 cassettes: **ISBN 0-87052-983-8 • $12.95 • (524)**

Hippocrene Children's Illustrated Japanese
Dictionary
500 entries • 94 pages • 8½ x 11
paperback: **ISBN 0-7818-0817-0 • $11.95 • (664)**
hardcover: **ISBN 0-7818-0817-0 • $14.95 • (31)**

Korean-English/English-Korean
Practical Dictionary
8,500 entries • 365 pages • 4 x 7¼ •
ISBN 0-87052-092-X • $14.95pb • (399)

Korean-English/English-Korean
Handy Dictionary
4,000 entries • 178 pages • 5 x 8 •
ISBN 0-7818-0082-X • $8.95pb • (438)

Lao-English/English-Lao
Dictionary and Phrasebook
Romanized
2,000 entries • 200 pages • 3¾ x 7 •
ISBN 0-7818-0858-8 • $12.95pb • (179)

Lao Basic Course
350 pages • 5 x 8 • ISBN 0-7818-0410-8 •
$19.95pb • (470)

Malay-English/English-Malay
Standard Dictionary
21,000 entries • 631 pages • 5 x 7¼ •
ISBN 0-7818-0103-6 • $16.95pb • (428)

Beginner's Maori
121 pages • 5⅜ x 8½ • ISBN 0-7818-0605-4 • $8.95pb •
(703)

Neo-Melanesian-English Concise Dictionary
1,900 entries • 160 pages • 5 x 8 •
ISBN 0-7818-0656-9 • $11.95pb • (746)

Pilipino-English/English-Pilipino
Concise Dictionary
5,000 entries • 389 pages • 4 x 6 •
ISBN 0-87052-491-7 • $9.95pb • (393)

Pilipino-English/English-Pilipino
Dictionary and Phrasebook (Tagalog)
2,000 entries • 186 pages • 3¾ x 7 •
ISBN 0-7818-0451-5 • $11.95pb • (295)

Thai-English/English-Thai
Dictionary and Phrasebook
Romanized
1,800 entries • 206 pages • 3¾ x 7 •
ISBN 0-7818-0774-3 • $12.95pb • (330)

Beginner's Vietnamese
517 pages • 7 x 10 • ISBN 0-7818-0411-6 • $19.95pb •
(253)

Vietnamese-English/English-Vietnamese
Standard Dictionary
12,000 entries • 501 pages • 5 x 7 •
ISBN 0-87052-924-2 • $19.95pb • (529)

ILLUSTRATED HISTORIES

China: An Illustrated History
142 pages • 50 illustrations • 5 x 7 •
ISBN 0-7818-0821-9 • $14.95hc • (542)

Korea: An Illustrated History
150 pages • 50 illustrations • 5 x 7
paperback: **ISBN 0-7818-0873-1 • $12.95 • (354)**
hardcover: **ISBN 0-7818-0785-9 • $14.95 • (152)**

COOKBOOKS

The Best of Taiwanese Cuisine
140 pages • illustrations • 5½ x 8½ •
ISBN 0-7818-0855-3 • $24.95hc • (46)

The Joy of Chinese Cooking
226 pages • 5 x 8½ • ISBN 0-7818-0097-8 • $8.95pb •
(288)

All prices are subject to change without prior notice. To order **Hippocrene Books**, contact your local bookstore, call (718) 454-2366, visit www.hippocrenebooks.com, or write to: Hippocrene Books, 171 Madison Avenue, New York, NY 10016. Please enclose check or money order adding $5.00 shipping (UPS) for the first book and $.50 for each additional title.